BISHOPS AND PEOPLE

By Members of the Catholic Theological Faculty
of Tübingen   GÜNTER BIEMER   HANS KÜNG
JOHANNES NEUMANN   PETER STOCKMEIER
and others
with
BISHOP JOSEF SCHOISWOHL
and LEONARD SWIDLER

BISHOPS
AND PEOPLE

Edited and Translated by
LEONARD SWIDLER
and
ARLENE SWIDLER

THE WESTMINSTER PRESS
Philadelphia

The first six articles were translated from the
Theologische Quartalschrift 2 (1969)
and are used by permission
of the Catholic Theological Faculty,
Tübingen University,
and Erich Wewel Verlag.

ISBN 0–664–24899–3

Library of Congress Catalog Card No. 70–121763

Book design by
Dorothy Alden Smith

Published by The Westminster Press®
Philadelphia, Pennsylvania

PRINTED IN THE UNITED STATES OF AMERICA

CONTENTS

INTRODUCTION

This is a book about the governance of the church. It is addressed primarily to Roman Catholics, but it will also be of serious value to all Christians who are interested in the renewal of the structures of governance in their own churches, and all Christians who are interested in Christian unity. In large part it is a translation of an issue of the organ of the Catholic Theological Faculty of the University of Tübingen, Germany, the *Theologische Quartalschrift,* which was specially devoted to a practical discussion of some crucial issues in the roles of bishops, priests, and people. All the articles, save that of the undersigned, were written by members of that Tübingen faculty; hence they are careful, scholarly analyses. However, they are also at the same time very pointedly practical in their recommendations.

The first item is a letter from Bishop Schoiswohl, who only recently resigned as ordinary of the diocese of Graz-Seckau, Austria. From his own experiences Bishop Schoiswohl reflects on what it means to be a bishop today

and on the possibility and desirability of collegial government, the election of the bishop, and a limited term of
office for him. The first article, composed jointly by
twelve professors of Catholic theology at Tübingen, very
carefully deals with the relatively narrow, but extremely
important, question of a limited term of office for bishops;
their considered judgment is that bishops ought to serve
for a term of eight years. Then follows the article by
Günter Biemer, dealing with the question of the election
of bishops. The treatment is very largely contemporary,
at times even reportorial, and not only concludes that
bishops ought to be elected, but suggests concretely how
this might be arranged, both in the long range and starting
from the current situation.

If the questions of the election and the limited term of
office of the bishop are to be seriously dealt with in the
practical order, they will have to be treated within the
discipline of canon law, for that is where the practical
regulations governing such matters are located. Johannes
Neumann's article takes these matters up within this
realm of canon law and concludes that there are no
hindrances to these two ideas in canon law.

Peter Stockmeier's article broadens the scope somewhat, which it well can do since it is largely a historical
investigation of the early Christian church. It deals not
only with the matters of the election and limitation of
the term of office of the bishop by the priests and people
(which were customary for many centuries in Western
Christianity, as they still are in many parts of Eastern
Christianity today) but also with something of the roles of
the community and the bishop in the governance of the
church. Hans Küng's article carries the themes of the co-
responsibility of the laity in the elections and governance
of the church farther in a more contemporary analysis
where a more synodal, collegial type of government is
argued for. Co-responsibility is called for on every level
in the church, and very specific suggestions on every level

are given. (Professor Küng's essay here is the slightly revised version that appeared in the *Journal of Ecumenical Studies,* Vol. VI, 4 [1969], pp. 511–533.)

The last article, by Leonard Swidler, professor of Roman Catholic history and thought in the Religion Department, Temple University, deals largely historically with the roles the laity and clergy have had in decision-making and the selection of their leaders in American Catholicism. The conclusion is that American Catholicism does have a record of legitimate and creative lay and priestly involvement in ecclesiastical governance and elections, but that it has been covered over by a desert of episcopal authoritarianism that only with Vatican II is slowly being dug away.

The message of the whole book is that co-responsibility is the mission to which all Christians are called today, and that for Roman Catholics this mission has very specific implications for changes in church structure, the most important of which are carefully spelled out here. These are not questions any committed Christian can let slide by, saying that these are purely internal institutional matters and the important thing about Christianity is to love one's neighbor and serve God's world about us; such thinking is a trap. Of course the Christian must be turned toward his neighbor in a posture of service. But Christianity, like any human enterprise, is not solely an individual undertaking, but is also, and essentially, a communal one. Hence, if a person is going to be Christian he must be vitally concerned with the Christian community that has nourished him and has given him the inspiration to be a "man for others." Moreover, Catholics should be painfully aware that it is only very recently that they have begun, and only begun, to come out of their isolation to love and serve the world about them; those Catholics who have been so liberated to become more fully Christian have a very deep obligation to help in the liberation and maturation of their fellow Catholics who still remain essentially in the ghetto and those who in the future will be born into it. There are 500,000,000 Roman Catholics in the world today and there will be many more hundreds of millions of them in the future; anything that can be done to give them greater freedom and responsibility within their church structures will automatically have a massive impact on the whole world.

There is a still further reason why Catholics (and their Protestant friends) desperately need to be vitally concerned with the structural reforms of the church discussed in this book: judging from past history, if the loci of power in the Catholic Church are not distributed among the various elements of the laity, priests, bishops, and pope (and not limited essentially to the pope and the local bishops—who are appointed by him), practically all the theological and spiritual gains made by Vatican II will be withered away! It has happened time and again before (see my discussion, "Renewal: Optimism or Despair?" *Journal of Ecumenical Studies* VI, 4 [Fall, 1969], pp. 620 ff.) when progressive elements have not been able to consolidate their advances with the establishment of political bases of power; and when the general cultural atmosphere turned more conservative, as it inevitably does, a few authoritarian bishops and popes quickly and totally changed the situation. Who would have thought in 1418, just after the Ecumenical Council of Constance declared the superiority of an ecumenical council over a pope and decreed that such a council should meet every ten years, that authoritarianism would again soon gain the upper hand, so that in less than a century the great rending of Christianity in the Protestant Reformation would be historically necessary? Who would have thought in 1830 in Germany, when *Aufklärung* Catholicism looked as far-reaching and as triumphant locally as Vatican II Catholicism did in 1965, that by 1850 almost all trace of those reforms would have been obliterated and a weighted tombstone put on them with the 1870 Vatican

Council—which was just one hundred years ago? If the progressive forces within Catholicism, with the support and help of their ecumenical friends, do not find effective ways of opening up the power structures of institutional Catholicism, they will soon find themselves covered over by the returning sands of conservatism. Then once again hundreds of millions of Catholics, and many others whom they influence, will return to the semidarkness of isolation, forsaking the essential gospel task of loving, serving, and preparing the world for the Parousia. *Tolle, lege!*

LEONARD SWIDLER

Lent, 1970

I

AN EXCHANGE OF LETTERS
WITH BISHOP JOSEF SCHOISWOHL[1]

Theologische Quartalschrift
Tübingen, Germany
February 14, 1969

His Excellency Dr. J. Schoiswohl
Vienna, Austria

Your Excellency:

For a long time we have been planning that the second issue in 1969 of our *Theologische Quartalschrift*, which was founded 150 years ago, should deal with the episcopal office and its time limitation. In addition to the scholarly treatment of the question which is obviously proper for our magazine, it seemed to us especially valuable for a man who has experienced what it is to be a bishop and at the same time also knows what it is to be no longer a bishop to add a few authentic statements.

It is far from our intention to approach you with this request for the sake of any kind of sensation. Rather we are concerned with the problem of the structure of the church and a genuine theological question from the perspective of the *Theologische Quartalschrift,* and thus, in view of the step which you personally have taken, we wish to offer you a serious forum in which, far removed from press sensationalism, any possible misunderstandings can be fairly and objectively removed. We are thinking less of an essay than perhaps the form of a letter, which could be formulated as an answer to an inquiry by the *Theologische Quartalschrift,* but which would provide complete freedom for you.

We hope that you do not feel this letter is indiscreet. We have decided upon it because a step such as you have made, and for which we have great respect, can never be merely private in the church. Should you decide upon a publishable answer to our request, it should be in our hands in March at the latest. If you can give us an assent, for which we sincerely ask you, we will gladly hold a corresponding space in our magazine free for you.

Respectfully,
The Editors

Wiener Neustadt
February 26, 1969

Theologische Quartalschrift
Tübingen, Germany

Gentlemen:

More than nineteen years ago I accepted the office of ordinary over a local church under completely different presuppositions than can be assumed today. In between lie not only Vatican II with its new signposts, which I completely and entirely affirmed, along with the great majority of bishops, but also forces which, proceeding from a renewed theology, have burst into the open and question all the arrangements of the church from the bottom up in terms of their validity and authorization in their existing form. Whether and to what extent they go beyond their mark I will not discuss here.

In laying down my office I emphasized that I have a high opinion of the episcopal office. This attitude was no small part of my decision to take this step.

I was quite serious in seeing in it an immediate commission by Christ. Today great studies are written on the various tendencies in church structures in the New Testament; and in every case a supreme organ of direction in the order inherent in every community, including the church, is found necessary. Nevertheless, I always saw as the decisive point the fact that the embryonic tendencies received information on this from Christ, which then—one could say, of necessity—led to the given development of the present ecclesiastical offices.

Of course it was also clear to me from the beginning that the episcopal office could not be treated like a sovereign office of the old style. Moreover, justice is in no way done to it by its overwhelmingly juridical descriptions or safeguards. It is an office of service, as the Second Vatican Council expressed it clearly enough. Its goals are: to introduce the great and small into the faith, to open the Scriptures; to awaken the good in men, to strengthen and to form the foundation of life through love; to lead the way in difficulties, to set an example of the liberation and exaltation of the self in participation in the sorrows of the Lord (in various ways); to proclaim that freedom which frees one from a life of formal fulfillment of the law and enables one to live one's faith with integrity, so that the Christian life will be seen as both humanly appealing and genuinely liberating; to be the conscience of the milieu, where the basic requisites of an existence worthy of a human being are constantly disturbed; to take to heart the signs of the times when, because of changes and progress, the thought models of men also change; never-theless not to fall dupe to the *Zeitgeist* in a cheap adapta-tion, but rather by discrimination to separate the chaff from the wheat; to stand, to some extent, as an example before the people; to keep in mind the temporal require-ments of life of those committed to him, especially the priests and religious, as well as those disadvantaged by fate; and with all this to be to some extent conversant with administrative matters, so that the church household affairs will not become a scandal.

This is a variety of tasks that each person can enlarge according to his pleasure. It is well known that today a bishop cannot look after this alone; for the most part he can only stimulate things, but in carrying them out he needs the many collaborating faithful, whether they are ordained or see themselves as co-responsible in the midst of the secular sphere. Individual tasks are necessarily to be taken over entirely by co-workers on their own respon-sibility, and of course not only in the sphere of manage-ment, the easiest task, but also in the areas of pastoral care, of the formation of faith, of theological elucidation, of ecumenism, of information. This collaboration occurs all the time on the part of the pastor, certain committees, episcopal offices, theological faculties, and individually appointed persons. . . .

Without doubt a mode of appointment, even of bishops, that met the expectations of the people (of various coun-tries) could be devised. Indeed democratic forms of con-duct today play an authoritative role in many parts of the earth. But they cannot be indiscriminately applied to the church, most of all because direct influence, as through a plebiscite, appears almost impossible due to the deficient knowledge of persons. Of course, limitation to the clergy alone contradicts the understanding of the church since Vatican II—besides, it is exposed to some group egoisms.

I could imagine that for special diocesan questions of

decisive significance a senate of no more than thirty persons could be established from experienced and far-seeing people, consisting half of priests, half of other faithful. The election of a senate would be incumbent upon the diocesan priests for the clerical members, upon the faithful for the others according to tightly circumscribed areas. Age, qualifications for senate members, and method of election could be established in the statute. Every six years, one half of the members would be newly appointed. Such a senate would offer the guarantee that its members would be entrusted gradually with the important diocesan tasks; it would also be able to acquire a certain knowledge of persons and thus would also be in a position to make a serious contribution in significant decisions. It would also be in a position to nominate candidates for a vacant episcopal seat, from which Rome could select one. Such an arrangement would naturally have to be anchored in canon law. The senate might be helpful as a court of appeal as much for priests as for congregations, insofar as it was a question of a forum for mediation. Judicial proceedings would remain reserved to the independent diocesan court.

Vatican II expressly emphasized the collegial attitude for the episcopal serving office. Collegial initiatives were created or the expansion of already existing collegial orientations was encouraged. Their development nevertheless proceeds most hesitatingly. This is the case not only with the Episcopal Synod in Rome, which should be a standing body with genuine competences and the right of initiative for all members, but also with the national episcopal conferences, which must also develop into even more decisive forces with broader spheres of influence. Individual ideas still primarily determine the plans of the ordinaries. The granting of appropriate competences to the conferences has not yet taken place because the conferences strive so little toward this. The collaboration and preparation by experts, which today has become obvious to responsible people in many areas, and which was so fruitful at the Council, has often not yet made its way into the episcopal conferences.

But when I speak of the collegial attitude in connection with the episcopal office, then I am thinking likewise of the collegial relationship within the diocese itself. It is not accomplished with "collegial" organizations alone. Priests' and other councils will be worthwhile if the fraternal spirit is not limited to individuals, or indeed entirely banned from the meetings. The "objectivity" of the treatment of a theme does not at all guarantee a human or pastoral response. Rather, only the reflective and ready openness to expressed opinions will create the climate in which brotherhood is possible, even on the pastoral level. But this demands an intensive spiritual togetherness that dares to express its own opinion and at the same time is prepared to acknowledge the arguments of others, to which all taking and giving offense is foreign, and that ultimately sees itself as obligated to Christ.

The same brotherly spirit ultimately needs to make itself visible in the entire presbyterium of a diocese. Not much is served by a good but silent intention. In an otherwise very noisy world the good must also make itself known now and again. Bishops are people too. If their intentions and undertakings are shoved aside unsolicitously by individuals, this is still no misfortune. But if the masses of people look on silently and passively await the result, an isolation can develop that consumes the elasticity of an—at least externally—solitary person. Brotherhood demands a loyal attitude, but also encouraging words.

There are also voices who deny the bishop the right to lay down his office. If he is called to this office, then he must dedicate himself to the end even if it is extremely burdensome. Some look upon a step of this sort as escape, as capitulation, as a scandal for those to whom the bishop was or should be a support and prop in their own difficulties.

In principle Vatican II spoke out for the possibility of a resignation from office, much more clearly in the discussion than it defined in the documents. The reasons for resignation could be of an objective nature; they could even be compelling. What arises from personal considerations will as a matter of conscience always be surrounded with a certain discretion. The majority of the communications that I received on the occasion of my resignation manifested a complete understanding of this. As witness let me quote one passage from the letter of a colleague: "Even this instruction (without a wagging finger) does more good and has a greater effect on thought and rules than a solemnly taken farewell, which you would certainly have reason and motive for. The people are very sad over this necessary step, and it will be a long task to cope with it. But I individually already rejoice because *you yourself personally* have set a limit on the totally energy-draining expenditure, and because you have so increased the luster of today's questioned episcopal office not only through a long effective office, but also in your departure, by which you have saved yourself and us the image of a diminished bishop handed over all too much to His patience: Only you could know this limit and we must (painfully) respect you."

I think I have said enough. . . .

With fraternal greeting,
Josef Schoiswohl

P.S. Be so good as to correct my errors in writing. I have no secretary and do my own work personally.

II

LIMITED TERM OF OFFICE
FOR RESIDENT BISHOPS?

by

Alfons Auer, Günter Biemer, Karl August Fink,
Herbert Haag, Hans Küng, Joseph Möller,
Johannes Neumann, Joseph Ratzinger,
Josef Rief, Karl Hermann Schelkle, Max Seckler,
Peter Stockmeier

I

1. "Office" and "authority" are no longer clear concepts with universally agreed on meanings. It is, of course, questionable whether they ever did have any such unequivocal meaning. Doubtless there were times when a specific understanding of "office" and "authority" was more or less undisputed. But just a glance at antiquity shows the variety of possible interpretations for these terms. And an ethnological and history-of-religion approach also shows the great stratification within this diversity. Concepts of office and authority are always derived from a definite social structure, which they themselves reflect.

The modern reevaluation, which can be seen today in an acute form, does not therefore represent simply a rupture with an unequivocal tradition. The self-awareness and the drive toward forming the world that have marked modern man have necessarily also characterized man the citizen. In the past two hundred years the citizen has not been content to think only of his duties; he has also become increasingly conscious of his rights. Thus a demand not only for justice and co-responsibility but also for a sense of service in office has increased to an unparalleled extent. Here it is interesting to note that in the secular area the general reevaluation did not take place until the nineteenth and to some extent even the twentieth century. We can trace this development historically. In Western Europe it runs from the French Revolution through the weakening of authoritarian governments up to the restructuring of states after the First World War, while the October Revolution in Russia developed the typical Russian form of Marxism. A new situation arose after the Second World War: demands for autonomy, joint decision-making, and individual responsibility were raised everywhere, and they were realized in a measure that is in part alarming, in part amazing.

2. Even some people to whom political thought as a whole was not foreign have only in the past two decades become conscious of the significance and force of the dynamic of this development which has been centuries in its preparation. From this perspective it does not seem strange but rather natural that any extensive critical reflection in the ecclesiastical world begins only after the Second World War. Critical voices before then were more or less silenced. The most diverse circles were at one in attempting to dispose of the speculations of the modern era as false subjectivism and on the other hand to install the church as the protector of authority. For centuries now, ecclesiastical speculation has been limited by conceptions of authority that have extended not only to questions of positive rights but to some extent even to decisions of conscience. Obedience, at least exterior obedience, was demanded and defended in the most diverse and sometimes most questionable ways. The man who combats such thinking is the man who has "gone through" centuries of self-reflection. Today this man looks at authorities critically. His criticism can easily become hypercriticism if it loses sight of its own limits and thus of the limits of

criticism in general. In any case, the contemporary form of criticism gives rise to a crisis that cannot be eliminated by external authoritarian measures.

3. Correctly understood, authority does not exclude criticism, but stands ready for criticism. Criticism is a method of authentic conversation for the purpose of greater effectiveness. But this says nothing about the criterion of criticism. There is a method of criticism that on principle criticizes anything that is decreed by an office-bearer. Such criticism cancels itself out; depending on circumstances, it leads to anarchy or to dictatorship. This method of criticism can simply not be regarded as a constructive contribution. For, instead of making a critical-dialogic contribution, it sets up an extreme interpretation as absolute. The authentic method of criticism demands that regulations be considered carefully, and that it be possible in decisive questions to enter into dialogue with those affected by such regulations; those so affected demand today to be listened to in a decisive way and thus to codetermine future regulations. A social structure that is determined by the old model of master and servant is outdated.

4. Contemporary man sees office as a function of society; authority, it follows, is recognized only insofar as it is prepared to justify itself through performance. The man who makes any kind of regulations today must always reckon with the fact that these regulations will be criticized. He must offer convincing reasons for his regulations. This is completely obvious to the politician and the statesman. In many cases a constantly reconsidered stance must replace custom-honored decisions. What seem to be obvious routine affairs can suddenly become problematic. A clear command will necessitate an explanation. A command will make sense only within the frame of a well-considered master plan. Dynamic guiding principles will achieve more than a rigid order.

These changes mean that the demands placed on office-bearers are being increased to the point that usually a man is equal to them for only a limited time. This rotation in office for the sake of the office itself agrees with contemporary social self-understanding and represents a key point of modern political constitutions. Even though one can apply this to the administration of a bureaucracy only in a limited fashion, still the need for the rotation of the top positions has clearly become self-evident. For even the accomplishments of years cannot justify later failures. Neglected criticism, acquiescence, and false respect not infrequently have had fearful consequences.

5. The crisis of the awareness of authority is visible not only in criticism of authoritarian measures. The crisis also touches the manner of procedure and bearing of those who occupy an office. "Office-bearers"—owing to the justified and unjustified criticism that is surfacing everywhere—have often become so unsure of themselves that they put their own authority in question still more by their insecurity and thus provoke still more criticism—unjustified as well as justified. This is how the exorbitant demands urged on many officeholders today emerge. The admirable combination of firmness and flexibility, of vigor in exercising power and the ability to make necessary compromise, is scarcely realized anymore. And yet the realization of such an attitude must be constantly demanded anew.

6. It appears that social-political discussions on office and authority also apply *in the ecclesiastical area,* that the Christian is indeed always a man of this world and time. The structure of Christianity, like the structure of the church, seems in many ways still shaped by the Middle Ages. Even in modern times the outdated forms are adhered to as tightly as ever. Some political concepts must be described as outdated, whether or not they may have been justified at one time. The principle *Cuius regio eius religio*—"The ruler determines the religion"—although politically enforced into the modern era, is foreign to us today. The concept of a state religion has become questionable. The person who does not matter-of-factly prac-

tice tolerance of other faiths clings to a medieval concept of order and is out of place in contemporary society. (Consider: there are Christians who look upon the statement on religious freedom of Vatican II as a great accomplishment!) In all this it is by no means necessary to evaluate the development from late antiquity to the Middle Ages in the negative way that is often seen. But we are confronted with the situation that the framework of the church and its legal concepts are, in the context of the contemporary image of society, part of a strange world of the past. They are not authorized by the gospel, nor by the structure of the first Christian congregations, but only by a tradition that arose later. This tradition, however, has become dated and today no longer suitable in many ways. We are not therefore concerned with establishing the utopia of a primitive church congregation. It is rather our task to test new demands and possibilities critically in the perspective of the Gospels. In this we must proceed beyond minimal concessions. Genuine construction is the result of a projected program and an entire overall plan that points to the future.

II

1. Office and authority are necessary; their significance must be affirmed. But at the same time, those forms still adhered to by office-bearers which may endanger office and authority must be reconsidered. Thus the question can also be asked whether in the future the *episcopal office* should always remain a lifetime office. Similar allusions should be understood as critical only secondarily, and primarily as constructive: for the sake of a correctly understood office and a correctly understood authority, new timely forms are demanded. Rigid adherence to traditional forms really seems inimical to office and authority, and only favors a criticism that in demanding a direct and absolute "democracy" questions almost any authority.

2. While it is taken for granted in a democracy of Western stamp that the cabinet and chief of state remain in office only a certain time, in fact only so long as they enjoy the confidence of the electorate, in the church bishops are named by the pope, and for life, or at least for a long, unfixed period. An old or infirm bishop can resign, but he need not do so. (It is possible to get the impression today that it is the pope's refusal rather than his acceptance of such petitions that is regarded as significant.) He can obtain a coadjutor, an arrangement that is understandable from a human standpoint but that nevertheless is not always satisfying for the diocese and thus for the church as a whole. The question of the election of a bishop has been discussed recently—in connection with the naming of bishops—with vehemence, though with no visible success. Yet it apparently has still been widely assumed that a bishop—named or elected—should remain in office the rest of his life. And yet, does not the decision to assign such an office for a lifetime conceal enormous dangers for the vital formation of the pastoral care of the diocese? Through such a regulation, the pastoral care of an entire diocese can be determined or at least greatly influenced in a very unilateral manner for decades. And beyond this: Does there not lie here a source of danger for the bearer of the office himself as well? The office-bearer is endangered by the knowledge that his power will continue for the rest of his life; at the same time he endangers this office and thus respect for authority itself by the one-sidedness—understandable as it may be humanly speaking—with which he exercises it. It can be asserted that the current regulation has proved itself through the centuries. It can further be asserted that any regulation that one lights upon will itself in its turn be one-sided. The question of whether the current law has *always* proved itself through the centuries, or whether history has not rather demonstrated the problematic of such an institution, should be set aside for now. Granted that such a view was

self-explanatory in late antiquity, in the Middle Ages, and even into modern times, for us today this regulation is no longer convincing. We find it questionable not out of a desire to criticize, but on objective grounds. That a different regulation—and indeed any other regulation—always brings with it certain disadvantages and is itself one-sided should not be disputed. The procedure should be to see the greater danger and the greater one-sidedness and to avoid them as much as possible.

We take no position, therefore, on the custom of the past. We do not say that the church was forced at the time of Constantine into a social order that can only be condemned. We see adequate sense throughout this historical development. The historically minded person should not apply the criteria of his time to other times. But he may demand that in the area of ecclesiastical sociology no decisions that are relative be given permanent, binding character.

3. It cannot be disputed: The present regulation that bishops be named for an undetermined time or for life conceals grave dangers.

But mustn't we make the best of this dangerous situation because, as can be asserted, the episcopal office by virtue of the gospel and also in view of the first Christian congregations can be understood only as a permanent office, and that means as a lifelong office? Or is it rather the case that here certain social structures understandably perdured, though they are not as such necessarily bound up with either the gospel or with the structure of the church?

In principle this question should not cause any problem. If Paul turned to the slaves and summoned them to serve their masters, nothing in principle is thereby asserted about the institution of slavery. The fact that in one Christian congregation, which was developing under the most difficult conditions, a time limitation on the presidential office was not discussed comes as no surprise. For the apostle himself this question never came up (here we would have to remember the expectation of an imminent Second Coming, among other things). The fact that it was resolved later in the perspective of late antiquity and the medieval order of society had very noteworthy reasons.

But these reasons no longer persist. Concerning leadership positions, there is much, in accord with contemporary civil thought, to be said for a limited term of office, but can such consideration or such models be transferred to the church? And even if it is possible, should it be done? Will the church not again take over certain political concepts that must perhaps soon be revised again? However, if the church is a community, then the forms of community that develop in it must be considered within a sociological perspective. That sociology is authoritative for certain aspects of ecclesiastical life, and not for others, can scarcely be disputed. In every community there appear difficulties of communal living that must be controlled by an ordered arrangement. Such an arrangement proceeds— explicitly or implicitly—from certain models and attempts to realize them completely or in part.

This does not mean that every new emerging sociological aspect must also find its expression in the church. On the other hand, just because old traditions mirror a certain social or constitutional way of thinking, are they therefore to be preferred unconditionally over new suggestions? It will have to be borne in mind that the problem of the structure of the church is not merely sociological, and therefore the most varied considerations raised against a new regulation must be tested.

III

This is our suggestion: *The term of office of resident bishops should in the future be eight years. Another term or a prolongation of the term is possible only as an exception, and only for objective, extreme reasons stemming from the political situation within the church.*

Against this suggestion will arise a series of doubts that must be seriously discussed one by one.

1. *Exegesis.* From the exegetical viewpoint no arguments can be asserted either for or against the suggestion. As the apostles proclaimed the message of Jesus and founded congregations in the most diverse regions, presiding officers were installed. The appointed office-bearers acted both as individual personalities and as a college. Then there developed—differing according to time and place—the so-called monarchical episcopate. That the taking over of the presiding office from the local college necessarily had to result in a lifetime term cannot be proved.

2. *Dogmatics.* The commission of the bishop includes a jurisdictional and a sacramental element. For a thousand years the two were seen in undivided unity, and then from the time of early scholasticism were studied in their distinctions. That there can be a real separation of the episcopal power of consecration from the pastoral power is shown by the auxiliary and titular bishops. Whether this separation is to be evaluated positively or negatively is a matter of opinion. The establishment of the episcopal vicar is aimed at uniting the power of consecration with a certain pastoral power once again.

Dogmatic scruples can be raised in regard to the above suggestion from two angles. It could be questioned whether the limitation of the term of office might not also seem to endanger the character of the power of consecration, so that the episcopal office would be degraded to a sociological function. Secondly, one could point out that in fact a certain depreciation of the episcopal office, which necessarily began after the aforementioned separation of powers, would be increased still more through such a regulation; whereas do not the most recent developments seem to tend toward canceling this devaluation at least to some extent? Moreover, might a new regulation not have very negative effects in view of a possible union with the Eastern Church?

None of the above arguments is compelling. The question of the character of episcopal consecration, which is certainly not to be taken lightly, is not touched by the above regulation. In the future it will have to be discussed further in the context of the problem of the character of priestly ordination. The temporal limitation of the pastoral power in the suggestion made here is not demanded arbitrarily, but, as must indeed be evident, on well-considered grounds, and in the interest of the universal church. And it is to this universal church that the pastoral power is oriented. Because no alteration of the structure of the episcopal office has been considered, there are no new basic differences vis à vis the Eastern Church either.

3. *Canon Law.* Obviously the effects of such a suggestion must be considered within the framework of canon law. The theoretical difficulties from the viewpoint of canon law might perhaps be formulated like this: If there is really a monarchical episcopate, will not its very structure be destroyed? For there are indeed consuls for one year, and presidents who are elected for several years. But are there kings and princes who are active in their office for a few years and then retain their title without being permitted to participate in the business of ruling? Will the whole concept of a monarchical episcopate not thus be called in question through this suggestion?

Of course one can respond to this question that in the strict sense the episcopate is not "monarchical," that the hierarchy can be neither defined as a monarchy nor transmuted into a democracy. But this does not solve the problem. For one must pursue the question: For the structure of a "monarchical" episcopate, as it has developed already in the ancient church, is not a lifelong term of office essential, so that to renounce it is to sacrifice this very structure?

The objection moves in a circle. The fact that in the time of the origin of the episcopate its official activity was not limited is disputed by no one. Nevertheless this does not prove that the episcopate cannot be limited in its official activity. Such a proof is necessarily impossible because the model of the monarch cannot simply be transferred to the bishop. Nothing of the hierarchical structure of the church is altered by a limited official activity. On the contrary! In this very withdrawal from the monarchical model we see anew the vital capacity of the church, whose structure is not totally democratized through such a mode of acting, but indeed is moved nearer to the contemporary political understanding without, however, being reduced to it.

4. *Pastoral Concerns.* The new solution would certainly also be objected to for pastoral reasons. There could be hesitations as to whether there might not emerge future difficulties even greater than the present. Two objections are especially relevant: First, the alteration in the episcopal office will lead to such inconsistency in the leadership of the diocese that in the long run the effects will be more negative than those of a relative—even if one-sided—continuity. A new bishop will get the necessary broad perspective on his diocese only after a certain time. And in the last years of his term of office he will be hesitant in many decisions because no one will know the direction or the attitude of his successor. A second objection asks whether the contact among the bishops of a country, and thus the work of the episcopal conference, would not be made still more difficult if the conference is constantly subjected to change in its composition.

It would be wrong not to take these objections seriously. Yet one must ask the counterquestion of whether what is here described as discontinuity cannot bring about—when seen as a whole—a greater balance. It is quite possible that in one or another case the above defects will be noticeable. But is it not better to accept them rather than to permit the necessary one-sidedness of the present regulations, which often—even with goodwill—cannot be changed at all by those involved and have to be endured for decades? And can such an "enduring" still be justified today, when we are subjected to swifter changes in the social structure than was the case in earlier times?

5. *Human Considerations*. But does not the solution given here simply run aground on human considerations? Can it really be demanded of a bishop in residence that he resign from office after eight years? Can such a demand be made when he has entered into the work and life of this office well? Is it not to be feared that those very personalities who are in a special way suited for an episcopal office will not accept it because they cannot conceive what role they could play in the diocese after their eight years? Today all those who still accept such an office can be pardoned for doing so only after great deliberation; will their willingness to accept not be almost undermined through this proposed change?

This difficulty too we concede. An unconsidered affirmative to the episcopal office is always undesirable. Perhaps in the future the phrase *Qui episcopatum desiderat, bonum opus desiderat* ("He who desires the episcopacy desires a good work"), up until now quoted mostly with irony, will again have to be taken seriously if such a task becomes humanly still less attractive than is today already the case.

On the other hand, one should not fail to recognize: It is the person who is convinced of the significance of the episcopal office as office who will also in the future most willingly accept this same office. And just those personalities who shrink back from a lifelong responsibility for understandable reasons will be able to say this yes more easily if they know that the term of office is limited.

6. And later tasks? One will not be able to expect the

new bishop to name his predecessor vicar general. And one will similarly be unable to expect the previous bishop to retire without a definite task.

But could a solution not be found here, if one could still count on a certain basic idealism? Would it be possible that responsible religious activity really could not be found for the former bishops? The question must be decided individually by the newly named bishop together with his predecessor. A period of activity as auxiliary bishop is hereby neither excluded nor established as norm.

IV

It is clear that in a consideration such as the one proposed here still other viewpoints must be borne in mind.

1. The above presentation refers to the episcopate. Inferences for the election of the pope lie outside this presentation and are therefore not detailed in this context. That even the pope for carefully weighed reasons can resign is, however, undisputed.

2. Inferences for the cardinals and the nuncios do not follow directly from the above considerations. The nomination as cardinal is neither theoretically nor historically bound to the episcopal office; a consideration of our suggestion would have to include many aspects, but none of these includes any special difficulties. On the matter of nuncios nothing can be inferred from what we have said. In the first place, nuncios are not resident bishops, and in the second place, one can ask whether a nuncio even ought to be a bishop at all.

3. A reordering such as suggested here would not be concerned with auxiliary bishops or episcopal vicars.

4. For the closest active colleagues of the bishop in administration, a time limit or a rotation should also be considered; however, this should be subject to the judgment of the bishop. On the one hand, the new bishop should not be required to adjust himself for years to a

staff of colleagues who advocate different interpretations on decisive questions from those which he himself advocates. On the other hand, it appears neither necessary nor to be welcomed that the naming of a new bishop would signal the removal of the entire group of colleagues in the administration.

5. More important than the question of a limitation of the term of episcopal office, it will be said, is the question of the election or the naming of the bishop. Perhaps this is also true. It would in our opinion be idle to argue over which question is more important. In the past years, a number of things have been said and written on a new mode of election, a broadened electorate, and the manner of ratification by the pope. The entire complex of questions urgently needs a reconsideration, which should not be shunted aside by an appeal to the stipulations of a concordat. The election of a bishop by a broader electoral body seems unconditionally desirable for the significance of the episcopal office and the necessity of its vital contact with the diocese, and it presents an apt setting for the suggestion of a temporal limitation of office. Throughout this there remains the possibility that the assent to a completed election may be denied on the part of the pope. But the possibility of such individual cases must not and can never be the reason for clinging to the regulation in effect now, which does not guarantee a vital relation of confidence.

It is, however, not the intention of the preceding lines to discuss this complex question thoroughly here. What can and must be treated is how to make possible the election of the relatively most fitted persons, and to counteract the random influences possible within the current regulations. While study at the Gregorianum in Rome should not of course exclude a man from possible election, it should nevertheless certainly not represent the desirable conditions for nomination to the episcopate.

V

It would be incorrect to try to see a pat solution in this new suggestion. Among other things it could be asked why the term of *eight* years is suggested. Why not five, seven, or ten years? If the responsibility and burden bound up with the office of bishop is taken seriously, even the span of ten years seems a relatively long time. On the other hand, a span of five years would be too short and as a result an uncontested reelection would be admitted and any further reelection would be excluded. Our suggestion here observes a certain middle course and seems to do justice to all the concerns involved.[1]

It could be that the chief concerns are not at all of such a fundamental theoretical type. Perhaps they relate more to the difficulties that could result from the activity a former resident bishop would later be expected to engage in. Here it could be pointed out that the suggestion is not at all so utopian as it may seem to some. If the former resident bishop is prepared to take over responsible tasks, a not inconsiderable burden could be lifted from the resident bishop. If the overall suggestion is basically worth considering, then this question is merely secondary. There is no possible solution—even with the best will—that will alleviate all tensions and be equal to all expectations. It can only offer a possible optimum.

The suggestion proceeds first of all from the conditions of Western Europe. It presupposes that—in line with the significance of the episcopal office—small bishoprics, often suggestive of deaneries or even of mere parishes, as for example still persist in Italy, would be consolidated. In turning to the allegedly completely different situation in Africa and India, the experts should first of all be heard. A carefully differentiated solution in this can be much better than one stressing unity at any price. Beyond this the future will show whether the suggestion in its present form cannot win friends even from among the opponents, who will first of all stress everything of positive value in the existing legislation.

To the bishop belongs in a special way the pastoral care for those entrusted to him. He has an authority that can appeal to Scripture and tradition; this authority is bound up with the structure of the church. But his office experiences its existential-religious ratification through an affirmation of the functions that are given with this office. Every office stands in a historical community and thus in a historical situation. The discernment and affirmation of a limited term of office seem to us to be a part of the awareness of situation and the understanding of office of today. The existential-religious touchstone today includes the readiness to give up this office after a specific time in the interest of the faithful and of the office. It is exactly through the fact that the officeholder, after years of responsible activity, would again return another form of service that "office" in its character of serving and in its power over man would be revitalized and again become credible to others. If Christianity is still supposed to mean service, the suggestion offered here should at least be seriously discussed.

III

ELECTION OF BISHOPS
AS A NEW DESIDERATUM
IN CHURCH PRACTICE

by
Günter Biemer

I. The Diverse Practice in Episcopal Appointment in the History of the Church

In the general current law of the Catholic Church the naming of bishops is done by the bishop of Rome as pope.[1] This canonical stipulation, however, is not an original given of ecclesiastical life. Even at the present time it is circumscribed or modified by a series of special laws. Within the dioceses represented by the German Bishops' Conference, for example, the stipulations on the appointment of bishops vary. In the dioceses of Bavaria, in accordance with the Bavarian Concordat of March 29, 1924, lists of candidates are sent to the bishop of Rome by the bishops and the cathedral chapters every three years, and additional lists are sent by the pertinent chapter upon the vacancy of an episcopal position. In naming the future bishop the pope is in principle limited by these lists and by the assurance that the civil authorities have no political misgivings on the suggested candidates. According to the stipulations of the concordat with Baden, which actually holds for the dioceses of Rottenburg and Mainz as well, the cathedral chapter in a vacant see presents a list of candidates in addition to that remitted annually by the local bishop. From these the pope suggests three candidates, and the cathedral chapter chooses one of them as the future bishop. The man elected is named by the bishop of Rome.[2] Still another approach is the method of appointing the bishop found in individual dioceses of Switzerland. Here there still persists a free and unlimited suffrage by the cathedral chapter, whose elected candidates are merely confirmed by the bishop of Rome.[3]

In the more recent phase of church history one form of episcopal appointment grew increasingly strong and extensive: that of independent papal appointment on the basis of submitted lists with the elimination of the rights of any previous preferential indication, nomination, or presentation. This practice holds in mission countries, in the United States, in a modified way also for some German dioceses, and so on. Klaus Mörsdorf emphasizes that this manner of treating the lists is in essence "a canonical suffrage emptied of its legal binding force." [4]

From the above examples it can already be seen that the church of today is familiar with a variety of forms in the appointment of episcopal candidates. That, however, means that none of these forms can be absolutely obligatory, that rather they all have grown out of historical situations, and that they thus would logically be modifiable by new historical postulates. This conclusion can be clearly verified by looking back to the broader horizons of church history.

From the history of the church at the time of the fathers two aspects merit special attention in this context: the participation of the entire body of all ordained Christians[5] and the active role of all the baptized in the appointment of bishops. From Clement of Rome on

through Hippolytus, Cyprian, and Celestine I, up until
Leo I, the patristic witnesses make it quite clear that the
differentiated collaboration of the entire diocese is involved in the appointment of bishops. So, for example,
Cyprian speaks of Bishop Cornelius, who was ordained
"in the Catholic Church by the judgment of God and the
suffrage of the clergy and people." [6] Yves Congar sum-
marizes the process of naming bishops in the patristic
church: The appointment of bishops was "the subject of
an election in which the clergy and the laity participated.
The business of the clergy was formal nomination, that
of the people approbation and assent, both under the
supervision of the bishops and metropolitans." [7] This
practice corresponded to the principle of Leo I: "He who
will preside over all should be elected by all." [8]

Various factors, among others the liaison of church and
state and the encroachment of the politically powerful,
led to the replacing of the episcopal elections carried out
by the diocese with a feudally structured appointment of
bishops by kings or by the great liege lords. The reforms
of Leo IX and Gregory VII, which aimed at reinstating
the old form of election, were of only short duration. The
exclusion of nonordained Christians as a whole from the
business of election at the end of the twelfth century can
be seen as an actual result of the centuries-long quarrel
between church and state over the appointment of bishops
in the Holy Roman Empire. The political establishment
was intended, but the nonordained Christians as a whole
were affected by the measure. In the course of this process the participation of ordained Christians was at the
same time limited to members of the current cathedral
chapter. This effort for an ordered regulation of episcopal
appointment ultimately led from the originally customary
communal declaration in the *epistulae synodicae* to a
central or centralistic naming of bishops—with the modified and locally limited restrictions outlined above.

This small amount of historical data cannot and should

not furnish anything but an insight into the historical con-
ditionality and relativity of facts that are often considered
firm and inalterable. But—and that is the point of these
preliminary reflections—they create a basis upon which
the newly postulated restructuring and reforming of episcopal elections can at least be understood and judged.

II. The Possible Effect of the Church's New Self-understanding on the Procedure of Episcopal Appointment

The question of the election of bishops, as it is presented today, originates not only from the knowledge of
the possibilities legitimized in history, but especially from
the church's new consciousness of her essence as the People of God. Thus the question has a firm basis. The conciliar texts of Vatican II, despite some equivocation, ex-
hibit clearly converging lines that lead to an active co-
responsibility of all ordained and nonordained Christians
in all the important events of the life of the church community. And who would say that the appointment of a
bishop is not an important event in the life of a diocese?

So, for example, collegiality proves more and more
clearly to be the decisive structural principle of ecclesiastical business.[9] The canonist sees in this the redis-
covery of a "characteristically proper legal order for the
church." [10] The pastoral sociologist finds that the social
expression of "dialogue, criticism and opposition as witness of the consciousness of faith" is anchored here.[11]
Practical theology can establish on the foundation of
faith, Baptism, and Eucharist a long-due, new conception
of ecclesiastical life-fulfillment, and so on.[12]

The conciliar texts of Vatican II give a multitude of
examples for the concrete realization of this structural
principle of fraternal responsibility, only a few of which
shall be listed here.[13] It is not only in the "prophetic office" of Christ that all Christians take active part through

their witnessing,[14] but also in his "priestly office" in the liturgy,[15] and in his "kingly office." Without the cooperation of the "laity" the "apostolate of the pastors is generally unable to achieve its full effectiveness." [16] The laity "supply what is lacking to their brethren, and refresh the spirit of pastors and of the rest of the faithful. . . . They . . . earnestly cooperate in presenting the word of God." [17] For this reason the lay person is "permitted and sometimes even obliged to express his opinion on things which concern the good of the Church" [18] to the leaders of the diocese and parishes. The congregational leaders should "willingly make use of his prudent advice. Let them confidently assign duties to him in the service of the Church, allowing him freedom and room for action. Further, let them encourage the layman so that he may undertake tasks on his own initiative," [19] and so on.

Such tones are new to recent church history. The person who hears them will listen. It should not be surprising if some people compose them into a melody that sounds rather like a new *"Internationale"* of a totally democratic process.

But let us presuppose that in the church there are also Christians who were not outdistanced by the Council, but are being overtaken just now, or not even yet. Let us also presuppose that the Council was a thrust forward and not a final resolution. With these presuppositions it is then to be expected that ordained and nonordained Christians, alertly obedient and aware of the distinction between *sacerdotium commune* and *sacerdotium ministeriale,* would take up the forward thrust and carry it farther. And the amazement that they should "express their opinion," give their "prudent advice," and exercise their own initiative on the appointment of bishops will be shared only by those who fail to see in the office and person of the bishops any essential channel or any important service to the church.

III. CONCRETE INITIATIVES FOR A RESHAPING
OF EPISCOPAL ELECTIONS

In the majority of cases initiatives and efforts to re-
shape the episcopal election have not resulted from systematic planning, but from concrete occasions.[20] The first
to take a step toward a new form may have been the
diocese of 's Hertogenbosch in the Netherlands. Bishop
J. Bluyssen writes: "When Bishop W. Bekkers died, our
cathedral chapter invited all the priests, religious, and
other faithful to submit their contributions for the drawing up of the list of candidates. The people of the diocese
were asked to tell what kind of bishop, what kind of person, was wanted, what qualities the new bishop should
have; they were not asked for names. Actually about a
thousand letters poured in (some from individuals, some
from groups). Often they described in detail the qualities
which the new bishop should have in these modern times.
In many cases names were also included. On the basis
of this information the cathedral chapter drew up three
names in secret ballot. The names have remained secret." [21]

In the year 1968 the idea of the participation of ordained and nonordained Christians of a diocese in the
election of their bishop caught on like wildfire. In January
there were 563 priests in the New York diocese who
asked to be able to choose Cardinal Spellman's successor
on a broad base of participation.[22] In February, *Le
Monde* in Paris reported that a group of Catholic priests
and laity had, on the occasion of the question of a successor to Archbishop Veuillot, directed a letter to Paul VI,
to the French nunciature, and to the Parisian vicar general, asking for a preliminary consultation on the naming
of their future archbishop.[23]

Likewise in February the question of a representative

participation in the election of a bishop was also raised for the first time in a German diocese. On February 13, 1968, the pastors and congregation members of the diocese of Speyer learned from their daily newspaper that preparations for the naming of a successor to the resigned bishop Markus Isidor Emanuel had been made. A petition to have a voice in the episcopal election, composed at an institute for pastors on February 15, was in a short time signed by about 23 percent of the active congregational leaders[24] of the Speyer diocese, and sent to the German nunciature with the request that it be forwarded to Rome. Whereas the chapter vicar of Speyer, R. Motzenbäcker, who had been simultaneously informed of their intention, expressed in a response his regret that, the seat being vacant, no innovation could be introduced,[25] the nunciature limited itself to a telephoned confirmation that it had received the petition. An indication of the Catholic press's eagerness for information was given by the reaction of the editor of *Der Pilger,* the diocesan newspaper for Speyer, which reconciled itself to publishing the news only after it had become public in other communications media.[26] A request to the chairman of the German Bishops' Conference of March 4, 1968, remained unanswered. On the other hand, the chapter vicar had received directions from the nuncio to speak with the initiators. The conversation, the contents of which are repeated in a statement of the Speyer chancery, was supposed to communicate the reasons why Rome had denied the request of the petition. According to it, "the Holy See cannot depart from the rule that holds for the entire church . . . nor from the prescriptions of the concordat valid for Germany." It was stated that in church history, for example, "Arianism was able to spread and to maintain itself in good part by the type and method of appointment of bishops . . . , that the simoniacal bestowal of offices and the misconduct of electoral capitulations could be surmounted almost exclusively only by the rigid centralization of the investiture of offices. Moreover, the Holy See wishes to create no new precedents. What it granted to the diocese of Speyer it could not justly deny to other dioceses. But then the very involvement of clergy and laity could be harmful for the church." Besides a "desire for a voice in the choice of episcopal candidates did not follow" from the principles of Vatican II. Finally —and this seems to the reader to be in unconcealed contradiction to the previous denial and its reasons—any alteration of the present custom in the naming of bishops needs time, because the matter of the concordat comes into play here.[27]

On the same March 11 on which the conversation occurred, there appeared in the press a notice of a communication from the nuncio to the chapter vicar of Speyer, which in part repeated word for word the same reasoning for denying the petition.[28] However, this notice had the consoling conclusion: "The Holy Father has the greatest interest in naming for the diocese of Speyer a shepherd to whom the clergy and the people can bring full confidence." [29]

In response to a new communication that the petitioners directed to the nunciature, the nuncio, again by telephone, invited three pastors to a visit at Bad Godesberg. While he had let them know in advance that the rushing into print had not pleased him, he also closed the conversation, which had proceeded in a friendly atmosphere, with the wish that none of it should be made public.

Of course this procedure of careful telephoned appeasement and paternal advice to be silent does not answer the question that was raised in New York, Paris, and Speyer,[30] and more recently in Cologne,[31] Münster,[32] and in Styria[33] in Austria, and which will perhaps be raised elsewhere.

The following somewhat simultaneous theological reflections on the new conception of episcopal elections show this. For a group of priests of the diocese of Freiburg in southwest Germany the establishment of a priestly and pastoral council was the occasion to publish in February of 1968 a resolution that takes positions on, among other things, questions of public information in the church, the co-responsibility of the laity and priests, the pastoral conception in diocese and parish, religious instruction and encounter groups, all in the perspective of theological and sociological analysis. In this context the writers were also concerned with the election of bishops: "The reawakened consciousness of community, the spirit of common responsibility, and the sociological structural change demand a radical reform of episcopal election. The present electoral method contradicts the spirit of collegial co-responsibility as it can and must be realized today. A broadening of the electoral college to a genuine representation of faithful and priests is not to be avoided. Alongside the episcopal vicars and the cathedral chapter, at least the members of the priests' council, pastors, pastoral council, and the diocesan council must belong to the electoral college. The work of a new electoral order, a corresponding petition to the pope, and the negotiations over the relevant modifications of the concordat should quickly and decisively be made priorities." [34] In a full assembly of the assistant pastors of the state of Baden during June of 1968 in Bühl, in which the outstanding problems of theology and church were discussed in five working groups,[35] there was formulated, among other things, a comprehensive resolution on the renewal of episcopal elections. "New Testament witnesses, the teaching and practice of the ancient church, theological as well as ecumenical, missionary, and social-diaconal reasons, speak clearly for a collaboration of the entire People of God in episcopal elections. . . . Reform refers especially here to the collaboration of priests and faithful, of the entire People of God in the search— which ultimately must be guided by spiritual criteria— for fellow Christians who are qualified for episcopal service, as well as in the choice of the future bishop; this choice is followed by the authentic commission and canonical *mission* by the episcopal laying on of hands performed by representatives of the episcopal college into which the ordained man is thereby accepted." [36]

In the "second Bühl Meeting" in November of 1968, in which the problem areas of authority and freedom, fraternity and collegiality, church and publicity, and regulations on assistant pastors were worked on, there was, under the heading "Freedom and Church Leadership," only indirect reference to episcopal elections: "Authority in the church serves the community; therefore the congregation for which this service exists should also collaborate in the election of its authority." [37]

Of the theologians, it has been especially Hans Küng, Karl Rahner,[38] and Norbert Greinacher[39] who have expressed themselves on the question of the election of bishops. In his book *Truthfulness,* Küng lists, under the title "Special reform tasks in reference to the church government," as catchwords a few of the essential aspects:

> There should be free election of the appropriate superiors (parish priests, bishop, pope) by representatives of the Churches concerned. This both with the co-operation of the representative bodies mentioned in the last point, in the whole Church (council of bishops and lay council) in the diocese (pastoral council) and in the local Church (parish council), and also with the superordinate pastoral ministry exercising a controlling and approving function: the bishop for the election of a parish priest, the conference of bishops or the pope for the election of a bishop. As far as the election of the pope is concerned, it is a matter of special urgency that this should be handed over by the college of cardinals—which is in no way representative and is in any case an anachronism—to the council of bishops and the lay council. All appointments to ecclesiastical positions should be governed analogously by the principles: "No bishop shall be appointed against the will of the people" (Pope Celestine I) and "The one

who will be at the head of all must be chosen by all"
(Pope Leo the Great). Election for a long but limited
time (for example, six or eight years with a possibility of
re-election) should be seriously considered in the present
situation, not only for superiors or superioresses of religious orders, or—as in certain parts of the Church—for
the parish priest, but for all office-holders.[40]

Meanwhile a member of the German episcopate and
the spokesman of the Vatican Press Office have taken a
position on the far-ranging situational and systematic
statements made concerning the reshaping of the episcopal election. "The representative of the German Catholic
bishops in the nation's capital (Auxiliary Bishop Tenhumberg) believes it is not impossible that in the future
even the laity would participate in some form in the
election of bishops. Such participation, Tenhumberg believes, must be seen as a further development of the
'ancient synodal principle, which constantly has comple-
mented and limited the episcopal.' "[41] Fausto Vallainc,
the spokesman for the Vatican Press Office, on May 3,
1968, said of the episcopal election: "There is nothing
objectionable in the faithful also expressing their desires
publicly in this connection. But any possible concession
must never encroach upon the right of the pope to name
the bishop."[42]

And finally, in 1969, Münster became the first German
diocese to carry out the appointment of a bishop with the
inclusion of ordained and nonordained Christians. Already on December 27, 1968, Pastor H. Huesmann of
St. Mauritz in Münster wrote to the priests' council that
it must seize the initiative, "in order that the person of
the future bishop of Münster would be ascertained with
the collaboration of as many as possible qualified interested parties, particularly the clergy of the bishopric of
Münster."[43] The justification offered in the letter was
that "radical tendencies in the democratization of the
church are not to be met by dead silence, but by meas-

ures that pick up whatever is authorized in these tendencies, insofar as the contemporary conditions of church-
state law admit." In the January issue of *Forum,* the
organ of the clergy of the Münster diocese, the head of
the cathedral chapter, Paul Wesemann, gave encouragement: "Of course we still do not know the day on which
Bishop Joseph will resign from the episcopal see of Münster in order to be able to dedicate himself entirely to
his tasks in Cologne; but it must be certain that the time
until then is not sufficient to make new canonical regulations and concordat arrangements. But we should use
the possibilities that we already have today. I could for
example think that the cathedral chapter would welcome
it if priests and laity of the bishopric would submit well-
founded suggestions for the list of candidates that it must
draw up." [44]

The communication of the moderator of the former
priests' council on January 7, 1969, to all the pastors and
parish rectors of the diocese also invited the nonordained
Christians to make suggestions for the election. Among
other things it stimulated a circular letter by the nonordained members of the parish committee of St. Mauritz
in Münster—Klaus Meyer-Schwickerath, Marianne von
Plettenberg, and Friedhelm Wacker—which was sent on
January 11 as a circular to all parish committees and
was intended to contribute to the formation of opinion
on "the participation of the laity in the election of the
bishop of Münster." The committee members especially
drew the attention of their colleagues to the special sense
of responsibility proper for such a proceeding. "If a
parish committee does not know of any qualified candidates, then it should not submit any suggestions. No
member of the parish committee who does not know the
candidates should participate in the voting. It is better
not to hand in a suggestion through the parish committee
than to suggest a candidate lightly just to be involved.
Should only a few on the parish committee know a candi-

date well enough to be able to nominate him responsibly
before God and the church, then it is better that not the
parish committee as a whole and as such, but only those
who actually are acquainted with the candidates, present
the recommendation." Thus the members of the parish
council had on their own initiative taken measures which
opposed those scruples expressed at the same time by
Manfred Breitschaft in an organ of the Catholic Student
Congregation at Münster: "The short time and the in-
sufficient publicizing, which permit no real discussion of
the question on a broader basis, make it obvious that here
on the 'lower level' of the church the democratic process
would be unsuccessful." [45] Over four hundred ideas and
suggestions were submitted for the preference selection
of the Münster bishop. These were taken into consideration by the pastoral council, which on its part transmitted suggested names to the cathedral chapter for the
real election and establishment of the list of three.[46]

IV. PERSPECTIVES FOR A CRITICAL JUDGMENT

Facts also are a part of arguments. In practical theology, the juncture of theology and practice, where the
relationships of practice and theory react upon theology,
the significance of facts is still greatly underestimated.[47]
Where it is a question of spontaneous impulses and actions, their legitimate compatibility with the essence and
the tasks of the church must be considered *a posteriori;*
for the wish may be father to the thought, but it cannot
without further ado become the origin of legitimate ecclesiastical practice. For this reason any critical evaluation of the present postulates for the sake of reshaping
episcopal elections must draw upon both theological and
practical aspects.

  1. The restructuring of the election of bishops would
be theoretically tenable in the perspective of systematic
theology and church history, if it is presumed that, pre-

scinding from a nomination by the pope, episcopal ordination occurs through ordained bishops and the unity is preserved by the testimony of community with the fellow bishops, especially the bishop of Rome. This is to say that, seen theologically, no objections to a restructuring of episcopal choice within the above limits arise from the essence of the church and of office.

Such an extensive change in the appointment of bishops is of course not the aim of any of the above-mentioned petitions and resolutions. All assume a centrally regulated appointment by the bishop of Rome and thus stand clearly in agreement with the statements of the Vatican or its spokesman in the press office.

2. Something other is the state of affairs in the practical area, which implies the necessity for legal changes. If it is demanded that the presiding officer of every congregation should also be elected in a representative way by the church or congregation over which he will preside, then there is postulated a new legal order of election of bishop and of pastor and pope. New legal prescriptions will be required to make concrete in a thoughtful manner the complex phenomenon of the desired representative elections.

In this context it may be useful to return once again to a critical judgment of patristic practice. According to the above patristic model the nomination of the bishop was the task of the clergy, and the contribution of the congregation consisted of concurrence.[48] Certainly the competences of the ordained and the nonordained Christians, their possible and necessary participation, must be considered and weighed carefully. But it does not appear theologically supportable to reduce the role of the congregation to applause.[49] One thing is certain, that the interpretation of the patristic witness in the light of Acts, ch. 6,[50] must see the contribution of the congregation not only in acclamation but also in nomination (of the seven).

According to the rediscovered principle of Christian

collegiality, which should also result in co-responsibility, a differentiating, qualifying method of election would be completely suitable for the appointment of presiding officers. Since the concern of the petitioners for a change in episcopal elections so conceived appears both theologically defensible and sociologically comprehensible, the necessary change of the present legal prescriptions should be a clear conclusion. The objection that such a new regulation needs time is obvious to any intelligent person. But such an argument would sink to pure subterfuge if what has been shown to be theoretically possible and practically defensible is thereby hindered. Speaking purely pragmatically, the change would presumably require only a fraction of the ability, effort, and time that has been expended on the negotiations over the Christian parochial schools or the new status of the Teachers Colleges in Germany.

3. In the present situation an episcopal election with a representative participation of the whole diocese is not yet possible. On the other hand, from the theological, practical, and legal points of view, a participatory decision in the preference selection is possible. Concerned persons could express their opinion on the desirable characteristics for a bishop for that diocese for that time, as has already been the case in 's Hertogenbosch and Münster; on the other hand, the form of the specific suggestion of possible candidates is worth considering. Both possibilities would be in the spirit of suggestions, as the petitions have been up till now, and could be combined with the following outline of guiding principles:

In principle it should be possible for all members of a diocese to express their opinion and desires on the character of a future bishop. Likewise all should be enabled to make a spiritually responsible and solidly based nomination of proper candidates. Such suggestions, which should be presented within the situations of a functional group,[51] would then be brought before the freely elected and democratically representative committee of the pastoral council for deliberation and selection. According to the conclusions of the assistant pastors of Baden, suggestions that emerge from the circle of the cathedral chapter could then occur on the basis of the lists of candidates submitted by the pastoral council according to the custom of the concordat in that place.

Thus despite the lack of legal change in episcopal elections one can already conduct a reform that affects neither the legally guaranteed election of bishops nor the naming by the pope in any fashion.

V. FINAL CONSIDERATIONS

The election of bishops is doubtless not the most important concern of the Catholic Church and its theology in the present and future. Anyone who has occupied himself with this question must be aware of this. On the other hand, it must be clear to any responsible officeholder in the church to what degree active, critical, and well-meaning members of the church are disturbed by this problem. One movement, the liturgical movement, has already grown in the church which could have easily been dismissed as irrelevant, esthetic, or illegitimate but which became an important component of the new consciousness of the church in the Second Vatican Council. What effects the theoretical initiatives and practical impulses in the question of episcopal election will yield for the fulfillment of the life of the church must yet be revealed. But if the legitimate measure of restructuring that is aimed at is achieved, this movement of collegialization will result in no less a dynamic force for the church of the future than did the renewal of the liturgical life.

IV

ELECTION AND LIMITATION
OF TERM OF OFFICE
IN CANON LAW
by
Johannes Neumann

Election as a method of determining an appointment
to an office has a long tradition in the church, reaching
back into New Testament Scriptures (e.g., Acts 6:1–6).
The Apostolic Constitutions directs: "*Elect* bishops and
deacons worthy of the Lord . . ." (15.1). And the First
Letter of Clement speaks of the assent of the entire
church in the installation of the men who served Christ's
flock blamelessly in humility (44.3). In the first two
centuries the sources that refer to the constitutional organization of the congregation are a mere trickle. Nevertheless the election to positions of ecclesiastical leadership is comparatively easily documented.[1]

The appointment of a successor by the still officiating
bishop was, on the other hand, forbidden by the canons,
perhaps not least because in this way the inheritance of
the episcopal office within certain families could be prevented. Strict as these laws were, they were definitely not
universally observed. This prohibited custom, revived
again especially by the Germans, was fought even by the

Roman bishops, and repeated stress was laid on the
necessity of the election by clergy and laity with the accord of the fellow bishops, or later of the metropolitan.[2]
All this is especially notable because a Roman synod of
March, 499, granted the Roman pontiff the right to decide on his successor. Nevertheless we know with certainty of only *one* designation of a successor: Pope Felix
III (IV), who died in 530, designated the Roman arch-
deacon Boniface as his successor in the hope of obviat-
ing political confrontations over the possession of the
papal see. Although this procedure neither had the desired result nor was accepted universally by the Roman
clergy, the legal validity of the papal measure was not
disputed. When at a synod, however, Boniface II, who
succeeded to office in this manner, likewise for political
reasons named the deacon Virilius as his successor, he
was accused by the Roman clergy of disrespect for the
value of the apostolic see and for the canons. He acknowledged himself guilty of a "political offense," recalled the decree of appointment, and burned it.[3]

As difficult as the execution and realization of a papal
election may prove itself in individual cases, the "designation" of a successor in this way has never again been
seriously attempted; the fact that election for the papal
see has persisted as the single method of determining the
person for this, the highest office of the Roman Church,
is not without consequence for our question. The tradition of church law thus prevents the bearer of the highest and most comprehensive jurisdictional authority from
naming his successor, and even today reserves this right
to a legally established electoral body. The process of
designating one's successor could certainly have advantages in individual cases! That it nevertheless is excluded
in the case of the supreme pastoral office is also eminently notable because the similar procedure of designation of a coadjutor *cum iure successionis* (with the
right of succession) by diocesan bishops did prevail,

after some resistance.[4] The Second Vatican Council expressly confirmed this possibility in the decree *Christus Dominus* (26.4).

From the argument that there must be only one bishop as pastor and father of a diocese, which, as we have seen, was used to forbid a successor within the lifetime of a ruling bishop, there followed yet another stipulation: that a bishop may not exchange his church. From very early times a change from one episcopal office to another was seen as an offense against canonical order;[5] later, when the relationship between the bishop and his church was compared with marriage, it was even viewed as "adultery."[6] The idea of the indissoluble bond of the bishop with a church was especially promoted by Innocent III (1198–1216). It is perhaps not entirely peripheral to note that such mystical speculations were used to justify the papal claim that the removal and transfer as well as the acceptance of the declaration of resignation of a bishop were by virtue of *divine law* reserved *causa major* to the pope.[7]

One example shows the history clearly: theoretically the episcopal office—like every other ecclesiastical office—was transmitted for a lifetime or without any time limitation. But that did not exclude the possibility that even bishops could in fact be separated from their office, whether through *resignation,* through *transfer,* through *dismissal,* or even only through *actual physical loss.* On the other hand there were cases where evicted bishops were constituted bishop *sub conditione* or *ad tempus* of another diocese until they could once again return to their original church.[8]

Although the transfer of bishops since the time of Pope Marinus I (882–884)[9]—especially in the metropolitan and primatial sees—has grown more frequent, the ideology of the marriage bond has dominated the description of the episcopal office even up to the present time. That this understanding is today less tenable than in earlier times is not only verified by history, which testifies that the concrete situations often proved stronger than mystifying allegorical jargon, but also by the present reality: the two most prominent episcopal sees in Germany are occupied by men who were transferred to them on account of their special qualities, but who nevertheless ought to be designated "adulterers" according to this ideology.[10]

The ecclesiastical reality must thus take a road other than that which the ideology of the spiritual marriage between the congregation and its leader teaches should be envisioned in the name of a greater piety. The church must go the way of *reality,* because the episcopal office for the sake of its function is subordinate to certain objective laws. If it is subordinate to the extent that objective impartiality is able to prevail against visionary allegorical jargon, then it may also perhaps be asked today whether the office of the ruling bishop must be necessarily assigned for a lifetime. If there were reasons in history that the church saw as important enough to ignore the reproach of spiritual "adultery," then there are today, in a new hour of the history of the church, perhaps also adequate reasons for a time limitation on the episcopal term of office. For just as the "marriage" of a bishop was a metaphor, so today his title of "Father" is in the same position. The Second Vatican Council began the attempt to define more closely the pastoral task of the bishops, "attentive to the developments in human relations which have brought about a new order of things in our time." [11] That means that the function and the meaning of the episcopal office are to be defined by its *tasks,* and not by sentimental but unrealistic speculation. Just because the responsibility and the burden of a local bishop have grown so great today, an examination is needed into the question of whether a basis for future practice can be derived from the legal tradition of the church —in this case with reference to the manner and way in

which a person becomes a bishop, as well as the length
of his term of office.

I. THE ELECTION

The current ecclesiastical code of law recognizes a detailed regulation of canonical election (*electio canonica*)
in canons 160 to 178. By canonical election is understood
a collegial formation of a decision to summon a person
to a church office or a definite task by the authorized
members of an electoral body.[12]

Except for the designation of canon 160 (which, dealing exclusively with the election of a pope, refers to the
special norms of the constitution on papal elections of
Pius X of December 25, 1904),[13] however, no ecclesiastical office is named for which an election was pre-
scribed as compulsory by customary law.[14] Rather, in
principle canon 152 advances the legal opinion that the
incumbent local bishop has the right to distribute the
church offices of his diocese as he chooses. Only canon
432 stipulates that in the case of a vacant episcopal see
the cathedral chapter is to carry out the *election* of a
vicar capitular within eight days. This regulation is in the
nature of the case necessary since according to canon
431, par. 2, in the case of a vacant see the fullness of
episcopal jurisdictional power falls on the cathedral chapter. The chapter, however, acting as a college, can come
to a formation of a consensus only by voting; in the case
of deciding on the necessary vicar capitular this can only
mean by an election. Of the "former splendor of the
possession of many prebends as a result of elections by
the chapter" there can be found, because of the past
tendency toward self-aggrandizement, only "certain rights"
which the German cathedral chapters still retain—thanks,
of course, to the German special laws assured by concordat.[15]

In reference to the possession of parishes, canon 455,

par. 1, of course ordains that the vested rights to elect the pastor should remain standing with the limitation, to be sure, that elections by the people can take place only if they select from among three candidates designated by the local bishop (canon 1452). Moreover, such elections occur very seldom, perhaps in the archdiocese of Paderborn[16] or in Switzerland.[17] [There are no cathedral chapters in the United States.]

While in the general constitutional law of the Latin Church the electoral right—not least because of the danger of political abuse—withered in the soil of the not terribly happy Western development,[18] it has been better able to sustain itself in the laws of religious orders.[19] In this matter the CIC [*Codex Iuris Canonici,* or Code of Canon Law] provides not only for the election of the male and female superiors of convents by the enfranchised members (canons 506 and 507, par. 1), but also for the far-reaching right of codecision by co-option (as in the admission of the novices to profession of vows, canon 575, par. 2). In the religious orders—"orders" used in its technical sense includes only a few groups, such as the Franciscans [founded thirteenth century], all of which were founded earlier than the "societies," such as the Jesuits [founded sixteenth century]—the election of the superiors, or abbots, is usually established in the rule itself (Rule of St. Benedict, Ch. 64).[20] Going beyond this, the Benedictine General Chapter, as the representative organ of the congregation, acts in collegial decrees: all capitulars who have suffrage participate equally in decision-making.[21]

If the electoral law in the Latin Church seems at present to lead more of a shadow existence, general remnants have persisted from a history in which this law had a strong, theologically supported ecclesial role; these remnants correctly reveal that this ancient institution of law can—indeed must—be newly invigorated in a new epoch of church history. "For in the electoral law of the church

can be found the influences that are able to formulate the
exterior legal decisions concerning the spiritual self-
understanding of the church, if not theologically and theoretically, then actually in fact." [22] If today in the political
and general social area codetermination has become a
basic political postulate, certainly there is also nothing in
the ecclesiastical area against welcoming back the old
canonical principle *Quod omnes tangit, debet ab omnibus
approbari* ("What touches all ought to be approved by
all") (Decretals of Boniface VIII, regula 29) in the summoning of men to ecclesiastical offices.

II. THE ELECTION OF A BISHOP

Up until the CIC came into effect, customary canonical
law gave the electoral right of an episcopal see to the
proper chapter, which was to elect the prelate.[23] This
general right was, however, not seldom limited either by
papal reservation or by indult of the Holy See in favor of
a right of nomination by the princes of the land. Eventually the—general—right (of the cathedral chapter) to
elect the bishop actually persisted only in Prussia, in the
states of the Upper Rhenish church provinces, in Switzerland, in Belgium, and in Holland, as well as in the
archdioceses of Salzburg and Olmütz.[24] U. Stutz[25] has of
course correctly pointed out that it was certainly not
simply the old rights dating back to the Concordat of
Worms that the secular governments restored in renewing
the electoral rights of the cathedral chapter, but that
rather a new form had been created.

In the case of the election by a canonical collegium,
the *confirmatio* belonged to the pope; in the case of a
nominatio by the sovereign, the pope invoked the *in-
stitutio canonica*.

The CIC provides that the bishops be named *freely* by
the pope (canon 329, par. 2); on the other hand, it
ordains that whenever the right of electing the bishop

belongs to a college, the man elected must receive at least an absolute majority of the ballots cast (canons 321; 329, par. 3). By this the universal law designates the right of suffrage as a concession, but it acknowledges this right, which rests on old tradition or on newer political arrangements, without reproach. There is also no stipulation, as there is in the case of (the right of) patronage, that a right of this kind cannot be newly established (cf. canon 1450). Although the Prussian Concordat of 1929 permits only a remnant of an election, namely, the choosing from among three personalities designated by the Holy See, nevertheless, thanks to the energetic help of the government, it has succeeded in "at least saving the basic ideas of election and in extending the same also to the newly erected seats of Aachen and Berlin." [26]

No canonical principles *against* a warranted renewal of the system of episcopal election by a competent electoral body can be derived from current canon law. The reducing of the right of suffrage, and the resultant reservation in favor of the unrestricted papal right of appointment, came about mainly because the electoral bodies often pursued their own selfish interests rather than the good of the church. Through new legislation, however, this difficulty can be obviated. The proclamation of the Council "that in the future no rights or privileges of election, nomination, presentation, or designation for the office of bishop be any longer granted to civil authorities" [27] cannot[28] be cited against an election by electoral bodies within the church. What the Council wishes is doubtless the elimination from the church of foreign influences, an emphasis on the necessity of her freedom from worldly-political interests. But the renewal of episcopal suffrage is concerned merely with entrusting to purely *ecclesial* bodies the election of their bishop (or their congregational president).

III. Possibilities in Current German Special Law[29]

A transaction as important as the selection of a person for an ecclesiastical office and especially the office of bishop cannot be managed as one pleases. The dangers of abuse and manipulation are too great. Here if anywhere legal norms are needed, and their strict observance is requisite. Thus it is legally as well as actually absurd to require that in the case of a vacant episcopal see general elections should take place quickly. Such "elections" on the part of nonlegitimated organs—even if in cooperation with the competent electoral body, to whom a partial suffrage remains—would only have the result that the election might be declared invalid, and the Holy See would then be legally fully free in naming the bishop at will.

1. Nevertheless it would already be possible today that in the vacancy of a see the qualified electoral body, i.e., the cathedral chapter, petition the pastoral council and the priests' council to present suitable nominees. Such a request is of course legally not binding, yet it might be not without consequence for the electoral body; in fact, it could perhaps in individual cases help to loosen dead-locked fronts within the electoral body. Ultimately a bishop should be supported by the confidence and the concurrence of the faithful, and especially of the priests.

In any effort to put into effect the will of the People of God of a local church, it will always be necessary to ascertain this will, not through a plebiscite, but through the existing advisory councils, i.e., the pastoral council and the priests' council. This is true for two reasons:

a. If these organs are combined correctly, they reflect the opinions of the faithful of the diocese, inasmuch as such synodal gatherings can reflect opinions. As the post-Vatican II church again begins to reflect on her original synodal structure, the organs useful for the formation of

opinions and wishes should also be drawn upon in such
an important question. Surely in the ecclesiastical area
there is scarcely a task of greater significance than the
designation of a suitable persona to the episcopal office.
This task should in every case be reserved to the synodal
corporate body, in which not only a certain stability of
opinion but also a definite measure of necessary professional knowledge may be presumed. In contrast to this a
plebescite nomination process is far more open to un-
foreseen chances and also to possible biased and destructive influences.

b. But what is necessary in such a case, namely, an unequivocal formation of consensus without factional squab-
bling, can only be attained by means of a definite electoral or advisory organ. In an expression of will based on
a plebescite, there is moreover a danger of dispersal of
votes; this would thwart the attempt to attain clarity
about a suitable person. And unlike in the political arena,
where the electoral candidates are more exponents of a
definite political party, in the ecclesiastical area it is very
questionable whether the most suitable or at least *a*
suitable person can be ascertained at all in this manner.

2. At the moment, the electoral rights of the former
Prussian cathedral chapter[30] and of the Freiburg chapter
are ensured by concordats, so that the Holy See chooses
from a large number of persons and submits to the
pertinent chapter a list with three persons, from which it
can elect one (Prussian Concordat, Art. 6; Baden Concordat, Art. III).[31]

Of course the chapter, as the actual electoral organ, is
not thereby prevented from acquiring information in any
way deemed fitting about which persons the competent
advisory organs thought were suitable and desired for
the episcopal office. It must, of course, not be overlooked
that this procedure on the basis of the present legal
situation can also lead to annoying results; for example,
the chapter might indeed be prepared to support the

opinion of the diocesan advisory councils, but the Holy
See might not put the favored person on its list of three
and thus forestall the cathedral chapter's opportunity
to elect him. Such a procedure would be completely
within the legal rights of the Holy See on the basis of the
present legal concordat: After "evaluation" of the suggestions of the pertinent chapter as well as the remaining
bishops (in the former Prussian dioceses), or the annual
list of the (arch)bishop (according to the Baden Concordat), the Holy See draws up its list of three from
which the pertinent chapter must choose. As it would
undoubtedly also be questionable whether the highest
church authority would accept a person suggested by the
chapter on the advice of the legitimate advisory organ
but not on the list of three, so it would be exceedingly un-
wise for the other side to endanger this remnant suffrage,
still ensured by concordat, by a procedure contrary to law.
That does not mean that the German bishops should not
expressly press the Holy See to assure the right of election and allow certain synodal organs to set up their
own regulations.

IV. LIMITED TERM OF OFFICE
ACCORDING TO CANON LAW

The right to be able to elect a bishop is then of special
significance if the term of office is limited. The other side
of the coin is that in this case errors are not as disastrous
as in life appointment. Besides, it is in no way proved
that more numerous elections would mean more blunders.
The opposite can be expected if the facts of the personnel
and state of the diocese are confided to the electoral organ,
which it is presumed will not be influenced by outside
political or social pressure. Diplomatic adaptation and
political considerations were also often enough not avoided
by the Holy See under the system of "free" naming of
bishops.

But does a universal time limitation on occupancy of an ecclesiastical office, especially the episcopal office, not contradict the principles of canon law as it has developed up until now? Is not perpetuity constitutive of the canonical concept of office?

1. According to canon 145, *objective* perpetuity is a constitutive element of ecclesiastical office in the narrow sense. In order, then, to speak of an ecclesiastical office, certain rights and duties, which participation in ecclesiastical power implies, must be attached by the competent ecclesiastical authority to an office in perpetuity. The necessary durability nevertheless relates unequivocally *to the office,* not to the natural person occupying the office. The offices of local bishop, of prelates *nullius,* and of pastors are moreover constructed on the foundation of the benefice system. They presume—not least for reasons of legal maintenance—a lifelong term of office. Alongside these there are of course also offices with representative or temporary character, which are exercised either *usque ad revocationem* (e.g., the vicar general) or for an interim time (e.g., the vicar capitular). In the present study they must remain outside our attention, although it could also be demonstrated of them that the durability of the individual *occupiers* of office does not constitute the essence of the office, but that the office obtains permanence only from its juridic quality. The durability of office is therefore to be distinguished from the temporal duration of the occupation of office by a certain person. Finally, the fact that it is legally possible to resign from any ecclesiastical office cannot be exhaustively evaluated here.

It may be more worthy of attention that the occupiers of higher pastoral offices in the area of mission organization, such as the apostolic prefects and vicars, are, thanks to the historical development of this office, as representatives of the bishop of Rome, legally removable at any time.[32] The office indeed as a rule was not assigned to them only for a certain time, to begin with, yet their occupancy of office is far briefer than that of a resident bishop. And, in fact, cases of speedy removal are no rarity, when the case demands it.

Finally, the Second Vatican Council on objective grounds did not hold it inappropriate to recommend that the bishops "offer their resignation from office either on their own initiative or upon invitation from the competent authority" if they are no longer in the condition to discharge their office properly.[33] The *motu proprio* of August 6, 1966, *Ecclesiae sanctae,* asks all bishops "that they of themselves declare their resignation from their office to the competent authority not later than the completion of their 75th year" (par. 11). Despite the fact that the "competent authority" for the acceptance of the resignation occasionally seems to proceed with complete arbitrariness, there is already a definitive limitation of term of office provided for in current law. In the form submitted, it certainly has its disadvantages: as an example, John XXIII, when he entered office as bishop of Rome, was already seventy-seven years old. Because of these cases in which the charisma of *kybernesis* ("administration") developed fully only in advanced years it can be asked whether there are not more suitable forms for a limitation of term of office: legally they are doubtless possible.

2. Besides this there is an ecclesiastical office that is closely related to the episcopal and thus partakes of its character spiritually and legally: the office of abbot, as well as that of the (major) superiors in (exempt) orders or religious societies.

a. The Rule of St. Benedict says nothing about the term of office of the abbot. Because it was assumed at that time that the presiding officer of a monastery held his office until the end of his life, this silence on the part of the rule implies nothing for our question. In spite of everything, this silence opened possibilities, so that in the sixteenth century the congregations of St. Justina[34] and Valladolid, as well as the French abbeys—though for different reasons—did elect abbots only for an appointed time. In the seventeenth century the English Benedictine congregation accepted an abbot for a time. The abbeys of this congregation have in their rule even today an eight-year term of office for the abbot.[35] In fact, Abbot Cuthbert Butler[36] deplored the formal limitation of term of office in his congregation. He compared the abbots with a fixed term of office to birds of passage, meaning that the limited responsibility is not compatible with the Benedictine concept of the abbot's fatherhood. As he saw it, it would be good if the abbots of themselves would always recognize when their rule was no longer to the advantage of the abbey. But because "you can't teach old dogs new tricks," he speaks out for a limitation on age and even for the possibility of removal of an incompetent abbot. As a pragmatic Englishman, to be sure, he does not carry the father idea through to its logical conclusions; indeed, by his suggestion to remove the incompetent, he clearly gives precedence to the serving function over the father myth.

In summary we could establish that among the Benedictines there have time and again since the thirteenth century been attempts at a time limitation on the term of office for the abbot. On the one side, the father idea, of course, in principle favors a lifelong term; yet on the other side, there are recognized difficulties bound up with the abbots who are superannuated or incompetent because of a too long term of office. The basic idea of abbot as father laid down in the Rule of St. Benedict, however, obviously obstructs any calm and sober discussion. Rather it seems in a way to make it a question of status whether the constitution of a congregation provides or does not provide for a lifelong abbot. That an abbot with limited term of office might be (and is) theologically, humanly, and even more, juridically, possible is disputed by no one.

b. In reference to the major superiors of religious, canon 505 lays down the rule that these are to be appointed not for life, but only for a certain number of years.[37] In (exempt) clerical institutes these major superiors are always, according to canon 198, par. 1, "ordinaries." [38] That indicates that when it is a matter that demands a personal contribution as well as competence for effective work, and the special charisma of leadership, the ecclesiastical lawgiver views a lifelong term of office as destructive and thus prohibits it.

c. It would hardly be an objective argument to refuse to accept as valid the comparison between bishop and major superior—who is always, at least in the (exempt) clerical institutes, also an "ordinary"—by referring to the special position of the bishop as father and head. In those orders founded since the Middle Ages, the emphasis on the serving character of the office stands more clearly in the foreground: The shift of accent in the "modern" orders and societies—together with psychological-pedagogical considerations—obviously means that the lifelong term of office for a superior has been abandoned. Today in reference to the episcopal office too the serving function, that is, both serving as a model and carrying out initiative and organization functions, has again become more consciously prominent. The decree on the pastoral task of the bishops in particular contains so many allusions that we cannot enumerate them here. From this it is clear that canon law raises no theoretical scruples against a significant limitation on the term of office of the local bishop.[39]

V. ON THE FEASIBILITY OF THE LIMITED TERM OF OFFICE OF LOCAL BISHOPS

The law must not only take care that in the pertinent societies things proceed legally and justly; it must also ascertain whether what is of itself good can actually be carried through without damage to the principles of justice.

If one proceeds from the fact that the episcopal consecration is essentially the installation in the holy office

amid prayer and the laying on of hands, then it is not
unthinkable in principle or even blasphemous for a bishop
to return after a term of office to the service that he filled
before, perhaps that of pastor, religion teacher, or professor. Admittedly, in each of those three areas there will be
not a few actual difficulties in the taking up of the old
activities once again. The psychological difficulties, however, we can pass over here, as tomorrow they may already have disappeared.

The manifoldly increasing problems of the church offer
today a broad field of activity for those men who as
regional pastors could gather together experiences and
difficulties: First of all, the distressing problem of the
"auxiliary bishops," consecrated *in partibus infidelium,*
could be done away with. Moreover, they could serve
their own church (or another) further in an episcopal
function. On the other hand, they could also take over
supradiocesan tasks. With their growing significance, the
episcopal conferences would need not only a secretary
general, but also a bishop or archbishop as president who
could devote himself full-time to this task. Why should
high supradiocesan "bureaus," which often may have
greater significance for the universal church than does the
leadership of a diocese, not be led by former local bishops,
where they have proved themselves? It could in fact be
suggested that the leadership of such a "secretariat" should
not be a rung for the intensely ambitious, but rather the
other way around, that recognized leadership in a diocese
should identify someone for such a supradiocesan task. In
such a perspective—at least as it pertains to our conditions in Germany and in other technically advanced
countries—both as far as the number of bishops to be
expected [40] and as far as further employment and support
is concerned, scarcely a cogent objection against a time
limitation of the episcopal service can be advanced, unless
it be that the one who has ruled does not wish to resign
his authority. And that would be a final—even if not

canonical—argument *for* a time limitation on this service of leadership, care, and love.

VI. SUMMARY

From current canon law there follow thus no theoretical objections either against the election of the bishop or against the time limitation of his term of office. On the contrary: The concept of collegiality as common responsibility advocated by the Second Vatican Council leads, if thought through to its conclusion, to the idea that at least the bishops should be elected by definite electoral bodies.

Also, the idea of a time limitation for the occupancy of an ecclesiastical presiding office is not entirely foreign to canon law. As we have already detailed in this chapter, the laws of religious orders recognize a basic limitation of the term of office of the major superiors. Current law, beyond this, not only suggests that local bishops, when they are no longer fitted to exercise their office because of age or illness, resign from office, but also lays down a definitive age limitation. Thus in fact already a limitation of term of office is stipulated, even if this limitation is perhaps too inflexible, thereby necessitating the many exceptions. Such exceptions endanger the essentially good and necessary ideas of the Council. Canon law in any case sets up no hindrances to a new and better regulation!

V

CONGREGATION
AND EPISCOPAL OFFICE
IN THE ANCIENT CHURCH

by
Peter Stockmeier

According to the current ecclesiastical self-understanding, divine law bestows on the occupier of the episcopal office an absoluteness that has its limits in the pope but not in the People of God.[1] This vertical orientation of the ecclesiastical office implies a sovereignty that appears legitimized by the character of sacramental consecration, and thus the historical dimension seems to be removed. In the course of reconsidering the basis of the episcopal office, however, the question of its meaning and formation in the various epochs of history is also raised. The development from the presiders of the New Testamental congregation through the hierarchs of the post-Constantinian era, who were endowed with civil honorary rights, to the secular episcopal princes of the realm in the Baroque period is determined by various factors, among which the theological arguments are by no means always the most important. Without succumbing to a naïve idealization, we must say that the early church does offer insight into governmental forms in which the coordina-

tion of people and office-bearers was very pronounced—
and to that extent it is cause for reflection. Of course our
survey is aimed primarily at historical findings, but these
reveal a theological understanding in which the appointment of the bishops lies within the responsibility of the
congregation. In a milieu in which classical democracy
had become foreign, the young church practiced completely democratic procedures, which obviously were
compatible with the principle of hierarchy.

A series of investigations on the participation of the
people or of the princes in the appointment of ecclesiastical officials has already focused on the "democratic
principle," and in fact was done at a time when democracy was not yet a fashionable slogan. Examples are the
essays of the Tübingen church historians C. J. von Hefele
and F. X. Funk on the election of the bishops in the early
church.[2] The demonstration of facts of course did not
change the existing system, and even the valuable book
by Y. Congar on the role of the laity did not see this lay
participation as a part of "the structure of the Church."[3]
H. Zimmermann too, in his study of papal resignations in
the Middle Ages (*Papstabsetzungen des Mittelalters*),[4] is
of the opinion that the practices of the early church can
"obviously be disregarded."[5] Inasmuch as the conditions
of the Middle Ages are not to be predicated of the first
centuries, this is clearly true. On the other hand, it was in
the ancient church that those principles were developed
and exercised which later were also authoritative for the
deposition of popes.[6] Primarily, however, the question of
community responsibility for the episcopal office did not
yet focus on the pope, since his collegial union with the
entire episcopate was a central element of the papacy.
An examination of the question of whether and to what
extent an ecclesiastical official, especially a bishop, is also
subordinate to the judgment of the People of God cannot
be limited in the early church to the occupant of the
Roman cathedra, but rather must be pursued on a broader

basis. The problematic raised is in no way lessened by this; according to current interpretation (cf. canon 108, par. 3), in addition to the pastoral office of the pope the episcopal office too rests on divine institution. The proposed framework merely makes it possible for us to focus on typical elements and procedures that illustrate the claim of the church community on a bearer of the episcopal office, but also at the same time show how this claim often degenerated to civil political control.

I. Responsibility of the Congregation According to the New Testament

The fact that the later office of bishop was not present within the New Testament itself shows the flux of historical development in the ecclesiastical understanding of office. Despite all differentiation of the structures of office, it is clear that in the primitive congregation the ecclesiastical office remained essentially oriented to the congregation. It is well known that the New Testament did not adapt the conceptualizations of the Hellenic-Roman official hierarchy, but rather characterized this task as *diakonia*.[7] Thus the strong horizontal orientation of every official duty toward the congregation cannot be overlooked. Without ignoring the grace of God, this basic understanding implies a co-responsibility of the faithful for the office-bearer. Extremely revealing in the matter of the participation of the people in the appointment of officials is the election of Judas' successor in the "college of twelve" (Acts 1:15–26). The appointment of the so-called deacons also took place in a similar fashion according to Acts 6:3—by a search on the part of the entire body of disciples.[8] Although the basis for abstract assertions is narrow, the participation of the people is clear; on the men of the people's choice the hands of the apostles were laid.[9]

Alongside this method of procedure in the Palestinian

church, the Hellenistic-Pauline congregation recognized an unmediated grace of God, the charisma.[10] Such graces bestow on the individual possessor a direct authority and a certain independence. "A spiritual man, on the other hand, is able to judge the value of everything, and his own value is not to be judged by other men" (I Cor. 2:15). Of course the charismata remain subordinate to the criterion of the building up of the community (I Cor. 14:26); and I John 4:1 exhorts men to test the spirits. Thereby a critical position toward the charismatic is recognized as proper even for the simple faithful, so that the charismatic cannot assert his claim in the church unrestrictedly. The orientation of the ecclesiastical office to the community even in the Pauline congregation is accordingly subject to the judgment of the faithful. On the other hand, there exists no doubt that in individual cases the office-bearers themselves by virtue of their fullness of power did authoritatively step in and remedy abuses (cf. Blutschänder); it is nevertheless significant that the community of the faithful as such is summoned to critical co-responsibility.

II. THE ROLE OF THE ECCLESIAL COMMUNITY IN THE PRE-CONSTANTINIAN CHURCH

The control of ecclesiastic officials by the community of the faithful that was evident in the New Testament remains vital even in the postapostolic church, although the episcopal office becomes ever more clearly prominent. The Didache with its stress on the faithful community inculcates a critical attitude toward the authorities: "Everyone 'who comes in the name of the Lord' should be accepted; but then you must test him and thus get to know him; for you should apply your understanding to distinguish right from left." [11] This judgment does not devolve on a single office, but upon the congregation as such; in view of the high regard that was due to the prophets, this practice has great significance. Although there is no need to bring in elements of classical democracy here, it is significant that the role of the People of God is seen as having not only a passive, but also a responsible function. In the critical questions of incompetence, of abuse, or of apostasy, the individual case is authoritatively decided less from above than by a clarification conducted by the believing community.

1. It is significant that we encounter this procedure already in the so-called Letter of Clement, which, as is well known, speaks in connection with the Old Testament worship precept of *laikos anthropos* (40.5). To clarify the confusion in Corinth the author went back to the ideas of installation by the Apostle, and explained in this context: "Consequently we deem it an injustice to eject from the sacred ministry the persons who were appointed either by them, or later, with the consent of the whole church, by other men in high repute, and who have ministered to the flock of Christ faultlessly, humbly, quietly, and unselfishly, and have moreover, over a long period of time, earned the esteem of all. Indeed, it will be no small sin for us if we oust men who have irreproachably and piously offered the sacrifices proper to the episcopate [*tēs episkopēs apobalōmen*]" (44.3,4).[12] The argumentation is obviously aimed at the illegitimacy of the procedure in Corinth, where irreproachable presbyters had been deposed. The criticism of the procedure thus refers to the fact that the congregation—or a group from it—had taken action against office-bearers who were discharging their duties well. The basic right to such interference is, according to the text, not disputed. In this sense, too, the canon-law expert from Tübingen, Franz Quirin von Kober (d. 1897), explained: "The disciple of the apostles did not dispute the right to interfere in this way with ecclesiastical servants; he only finds it blameworthy that the Christians in these cases had brought this authority to bear against the completely blameless, and on this ac-

count he immediately added the demand that those dis-
charged be restored and the originators of the unrest
again subordinate themselves to them." [13] The congregation's claim to pass judgment on the exercise of the
service corresponds with their right to appoint the office-
bearers. Thus the Letter of Clement also speaks of the
assent of the entire congregation (*suneudokēsasēs tēs
ekklēsias pasēs*) in this proceeding (44.3), doubtless following New Testament practice.[14] This method of election
does not exempt the elected from any further criticism by
the community of believers; although the writer remains
cool toward their particular structures,[15] their responsibility for service in the church is not disregarded. For the
rest, the letter gives no further information on the theological question of the significance of ordination and its
divine character. It obviously offers no obstacle to placing
a time limitation on the serving office in the church.

2. For our investigation into the responsibility the
People of God have for their office-bearers, Cyprian of
Carthage (d. 254) is especially informative because in
him the episcopal-hierarchical self-consciousness was
particularly prominent.[16] H. von Campenhausen is correct
in emphasizing that Cyprian as a theologian of the ancient
church knew "no absolute concept of office, no abstract
abilities and detached privileges that belonged to the
office-bearer because of his position and for his own sake,
but everything pertaining to office still stood in immediate
experiential connection with the sanctified life of the
congregation and its various needs." [17] The involvement
of the bishop with the ecclesiastical community underlines the horizontal line of this understanding of office.
Although Cyprian is at pains to elevate the authority of
the bishop,[18] he by no means withdraws the congregation's
right to collaborate actively in the election and to decide
on a candidate by recognition or rejection.[19] H. von
Campenhausen reduces the role of the congregation in
the elevation of the bishop too drastically when he says:

"The people are merely present at the act of election and can express their desires and their approbation." [20] The witnesses cited attribute to the people more than a role of acclamation. For example, in his fifty-fifth letter, on the elevation of the Roman bishop Cornelius, after the reference to the function of the episcopal office companions, Cyprian stated: "Moreover, Cornelius was made bishop by the judgment of God and of His Christ, by the testimony of almost all people who were then present, and by the assembly of ancient priests and good men, when no one had been made so before him, when the place of Fabian, that is, when the place of Peter and the degree of the sacerdotal throne, was vacant." [21] The text describes the participation of the people as *suffragium,* which term means the voting of the citizens in the electoral committee (*comitia*).[22] While C. J. von Hefele on the basis of this term speaks of a "kind of suffrage" of *fraternitas,*[23] F. X. Funk declares, "The passages in their entirety leave no doubt that the congregation had not only a right to suggest but a right to elect in the full sense of the word." [24] In addition, the context so deals with the legitimacy of the elevation of Cornelius that the very design of the statement shows that the legitimacy of the incident is intended. Of course the intention of Cyprian is unmistakably to draw attention to the role of the bishop;[25] but here where he is reporting the orderly course of an elevation, the decisive function of the people is clearly described. This same conclusion can be drawn from the portrayal of the installation of Bishop Sabinus: "On the basis of the voting of the entire congregation and of the judgment of the bishops who had personally come and those who had expressed themselves on him in a letter to you, hands were laid on him and the episcopal office was handed over to him in place of Basilides." [26] In this "legally performed installation" [27] the constitutive role of the people is also clearly mentioned. The case of Bishop Basilides is noteworthy for the fact that he had lost his episcopal see

through a "legitimate deposition." [28] With his colleague
Martial he had been guilty of a betrayal of the faith and
other transgressions. Cyprian for his part appealed to the
people to force the removal of Basilides. "For this reason
a congregation that obeys the commandments of the Lord
and fears God must also separate itself from a sinful
presiding officer and it must not take part in the sacrifice
of a godless priest, for to it especially belongs the power
(*potestam*) to choose worthy bishops or to reject unworthy ones." [29] On the basis of their active role in episcopal elevations the people should also be active in deposition,
of course more in the sense of a rejection of the unlawful
occupant than through a juridical procedure, which lies
primarily within the responsibility of the neighboring
bishops. The possibility of removal, in any case, is beyond question. In the case of Basilides the fact is significant that he voluntarily laid down his episcopal office
(*episcopatum pro conscientiae suae uulnere sponte de-
ponens*) and desired to become a member of the ecclesiastical community as a layman (*satis gratulans si sibi uel
laico communicare contingeret*).[30] When Basilides later
attempted to have himself restored to office in Rome,
Cyprian raised no objection against the original intention
of the Spanish bishop to return to the "lay state"; clearly
neither a theological nor a legal hindrance stood in the
way of such a resolve. Indeed the legitimate ordination of
his successor cannot be reversed, and not just because of
the "consecration" he received, but also because of the
proper installation in his office, which obligated him to the
congregation. The sacerdotal character of the ordained
priest, according to Cyprian, does not exist in isolation, but
in orientation to service for the People of God and in
them—functionally, that is;[31] it is lost if the ordained fails
in his office.

3. This contradiction between the bearers and the
demands of an office necessarily urges us to reflect on the
merit of the person (cf. Titus 1:7). Even in Cyprian's

argumentation this problematic comes up in the background of the discussion. It also animates Hippolytus' polemic against the Roman bishop Callistus, whom he reproaches: "He was of the opinion that a bishop must not be deposed if he sinned, even if it be unto death." [32] The problem of Christian sin encroaches on the understanding of office here where the radical thesis of the sanctity of the officeholder calls the office as such into question. Hippolytus advocated the idea that moral failure brought forfeiture of office; this conclusion had already led to tensions in the ancient church, inasmuch as the charismatic was made the criterion of the institutional. The carrying through of such a claim would, of course, tend toward disengagement from the universal church,[33] while the universal church sought to clarify the problem through her process of penance.[34] The peculiar tension between human credibility and the official person of course also continued to exist.

4. A new element in the procedure of episcopal deposition can be seen in the process against Paul of Samosata. Having exercised a kind of governorship under Queen Zenobia of Palmyra concomitantly with his ecclesiastical service, he was finally deposed at a synod in Antioch in 268. Besides his theological errors,[35] the report on his condemnation also mentioned the fact that "in opposition to the disciples of Christ he had erected for himself a platform and a high throne." [36] Despite the deposition by the synod of 268, Paul nevertheless managed to hold his ground for more than three years, presumably because Zenobia was able to support her official against his accusers. After the overthrow of the Queen of Palmyra (272) the situation deteriorated for the recalcitrant bishop. According to the report of Eusebius, "the matter was referred to the Emperor Aurelian, who decided completely fairly in the matter, as he commanded that the house be given up to him with whom the Christian bishops of Italy and Rome had written communication. Thus Paul of

Samosata was, to his great dishonor, driven out of the church by the secular power." [37] This proceeding, even if it is unclear in the details of its motivation, presents something new, inasmuch as it is not the responsibility of the faithful that is appealed to, but the secular civil authority. By this step the instability of the previous practice could be checked and emphatic recognition procured for synodal decrees, though only with the surrender of co-responsibility on the part of the universal church. In Eusebius' view, this cooperation of church and state in the deposition of a bishop anticipated later developments. Certainly the "secular arm" of the emperor being employed for the church cannot yet be discerned therein; but, on the other hand, the statement that Aurelian had Paul of Samosata "removed solely on political grounds" [38] is inadequate, for in this case the emperor had probably become directly involved; that is, he pursued his own interest. It is easier to accept the idea that the emperor saw in the "appeal" of the bishops a welcome opportunity to interfere with the inner structure of the church. And Eusebius' reference to the criterion of community with Rome—of course in the sense of political, civil unity, not ecclesiastical unity—in no way is extraordinary. Even if the powerless members of the synod also brought political motives into the situation, in order to drive the condemned bishop out of the episcopal house of Antioch with the aid of the civil power, yet the intervention by the emperor clearly shows how the solution to intrachurch problems was sought. The deposition of a bishop can of course be pronounced by a synod, but it cannot be pressed to conclusion when the bishop is a potentate. To settle the matter, Cyprian still appealed to the responsibility of the people; in the case of Paul of Samosata the synod members made use of the ruler to accomplish the deposition in fact. This step introduced a development that, after civil recognition, led to a close cooperation between church and ruler, but at the same time reduced the people to the position of wards of the state.

Only when the harmony between the partners was disturbed was the responsibility of the people appealed to.

III. Assimilation Into the Civil Law in the Church of Late Antiquity

The recognition of the Christian church and its increasing privileges in the post-Constantinian era led to an amalgamation with the civil and social structure of the milieu which can be clearly seen in the area of law. The institution of *audientia episcopalis,* for example, enabled the ecclesiastical officials to act as judges even in public concerns.[39] So it is not surprising if, as a result of ancient thought on the ruler's responsibility for religion, Christians also approached the emperor and sought judicial decisions. The potentialities of Roman law were used by the community of believers to clarify intrachurch problems: this meant that the influence of civil power was necessarily intensified at the expense of the community.

1. The earliest example of such a proceeding is the appeal of the Donatists to Constantine. After the death of Mensurius, the deacon Caecilianus was consecrated bishop of Carthage.[40] His opponents declared this proceeding invalid, and of course one of the reasons was that he was ordained by a "traitor." When the governor Anullinus on the mandate of Constantine began to carry out the Milanese resolutions and not only restored to the Christians their confiscated property but also announced the grant of money and privileges to the elected bishop of Carthage together with the clergy, the resistance of the opposition rose. Accompanied by a throng of people, a delegation of the *pars Maiorini* appeared before the proconsul and delivered two *libelli,* one of which contained the accusations against Caecilianus, and the other of which expressed the request that the emperor Constantine would appoint French bishops as judges in the struggle in the African church.[41] Thus in the normal course of law a proceeding

involving the emperor, which at basis concerned problems internal to the church, was initiated. Later on, Augustine too criticized the Donatists several times for being the first to appeal to the secular forum, instead of procuring an ecclesiastical arbitration.[42] Constantine of course did not initiate the legal process himself, but appointed, as the accusation requested, three French bishops and Miltiades of Rome as *judices;*[43] he decided on the capital city as the place for the court. The decision of this court, which assembled on October 2, 313, did not of course fulfill the expectations of the schismatics, and they appealed once again to the emperor. Constantine, in accord with Roman legal practice, accepted the appeal and instigated a second procedure, which was appointed for August 1, 314, in Arles;[44] but this court too disallowed the accusation of the Donatists.[45]

The verdict of Arles of course was not able to clarify the confusion of the African church. While the Donatists made their grievances dependent on the emperor, they did not succeed in fully utilizing either the legal possibilities in their own interest or the distinction between an intra-church problematic and a civil proceeding involving the universal church. The appointment of an episcopal judge on the part of the emperor betrays his sense about affairs proper to Christian faith; the incompetency of the church to resolve its tensions itself made it unmistakably necessary for him in the future to enter in actively, for which action the ancient Roman unity of religion and state offered legitimation. Both this self-understanding and the church's assimilation into the legal practice of the Roman state secured for the secular power a high measure of influence in the summoning and also the deposition of ecclesiastical office-bearers.

2. Corresponding to the claim of the congregation is the responsibility of the ecclesiastical office-bearers in the sense of *diakonia* to the faithful. Where this service was no longer assured, in acceptable form, a bishop could be

removed,[46] with the procedure lying primarily in the hands of the synod or the provincial bishops.[47] Nevertheless, it is amazing that such an occurrence was not managed and decided only by peers, much less by superiors, but that rather the congregation had the right to participate actively. To be sure, the letters of Cyprian already reaffirm that the role of the people in such a procedure was legally un-clarified, a situation that certainly led to sundry disad-vantages and therefore bespoke the need of a clear legal proceeding. But for all that, the consciousness was never lost that the bishop is essentially oriented to the congrega-tion and somehow also subject to its will. In actuality, however, the supremacy of the state more and more pre-vailed, enforcing ecclesiastical resolutions and expelling bishops in the service of "the true religion." [48]

a. Canon 18 of the Synod of Ancyra (314) is charac-teristic of the "sovereignty" of the Christian people; in reference to the difficulties that result from the suffrage of the congregation, it ordains the following: "If bishops who are elected, but not by the parish for which they were named, are not accepted and attempt to enter another parish to do violence to the bishops installed there and to stir up unrest against them, then they should be excluded from the community. But if such (elected and not ac-cepted bishops) wish to remain in the presbyterium where they had previously been priests, then they should not for-feit their dignity ($\mu\grave{\eta}$ $\alpha\pi o\beta\acute{a}\lambda\lambda\epsilon\sigma\theta\alpha\iota$ $\alpha\upsilon\tauo\grave{\upsilon}s$ $\tau\eta s$ $\tau\iota\mu\eta s$). How-ever, if they agitate divisively against the local bishop, then they should be deprived of the honor of the presby-terium and excluded (from the church)." [49] Thus in the case in which a bishop is chosen for a certain diocese, but not accepted by it, the assembly espouses the cause of the congregation. Even if the difficulties in the appointment of ecclesiastical office-bearers and their subjective interests are taken into consideration, the downgrading of the legal claims of the elected bishop vis à vis the people is—com-pletely apart from the theological dimension—a mark of recognition of the constitutive role of the ecclesiastical community. It is the will of the congregation, not the office-bearer, that forms the criterion for decision in contested situations; only a return to his previous presbyterium is recommended to the office-bearer.

b. Unquestionably, the stipulation of canon 18 of the Synod of Ancyra resulted in a kind of uncertainty for the bishops, inasmuch as they had constantly to reckon with the critical objections of their congregations. The case of John Chrysostom is very instructive concerning the self-understanding of an ecclesiastical office-bearer in such a situation; he was elevated to the patriarchal see of Constantinople by a ruse; precisely because he had an extraordinarily high opinion of the priesthood,[50] his statements on his readiness to retire from an ecclesiastical office sound so much the more amazing.

He defended himself during his preaching in Antioch against the reproach of injustice: "If you expect it on our part, then we are prepared to resign from the presiding office in favor of whomever you desire; only let there be unity in the church." [51] Although it is not the episcopal office that is in question, the basic readiness to resign from a commissioned post in the church is nevertheless informative not only of Chrysostom's character, but also of his understanding of ecclesiastical office. He introduces no arguments—either from church politics or theology—to defend his position or to interpret it as irrevocable. Rather, he is prepared to acknowledge the voice of the people as the decisive judgment and to draw the consequences from it. Doubtlessly, in this proceeding the practice of the first centuries had an effect; as the bishop of Constantinople, Chrysostom of course also set out with authority to create order in his ecclesiastical province.[52]

In his writing on the priesthood, Chrysostom then came to grips with the ambition for ecclesiastical offices, partly with the intention of explaining his own conduct. On this subject, he states that despite all the glorious words about the priesthood, it is not unalterably coupled to an ecclesiastical office. Only on the basis of this presupposition can we understand his reference that a bitter bondage awaits those who quail and tremble at the thought that they might be deposed from their office.[53] Their psychological problems and wavering characters arise from the possibility of a change in office. Somewhat pathetically, Chrysostom recalls the heroic courage of the soldiers and their readiness to die and adds, "So too should those who succeed to this office be prepared to fill it and also to lay it down, as is proper for Christian men, who ought to be convinced that such an abdication yields no less a crown than the exercise of the office itself." [54] According to these words, which undoubtedly were aimed against the self-complacency of some hierarchs, office in the church is not an unrelinquishable power. In the readiness to resign from an office Chrysostom sees a characteristic of Christian existence, and his fate underlines this note. Certainly the assertion is aimed less at the theological question of the function of office than at the practical and moral attitude of the occupant; the appeal nevertheless is thinkable only with the presupposition that in the church an office can be limited in duration.

These witnesses from the early church make it clear, on the one hand, that the bishops were not simply placed at the head of the faithful, but that the people themselves were to a certain extent participants in the appointment of office-bearers.[55] On the other hand, the congregation exercised a certain control over their bishops, in that they could also be active in the matter of removal. In this situation the role of the people seems legally unclarified, so that from this point on, the dominant influence of the synods, and later of civil power, is understandable. In this development there can be seen to an increasing extent the reduction of the congregation's responsible claim on the office-bearers, which reduction at once led to tensions with the secular authorities. Obviously, as the young church sought under the claim of revelation to develop in a pragmatic manner, its constitutional structure and current situation as well as the examples in the secular environment had their effect. What cannot be overlooked in the young church, in any case, is the strong position of the entire congregation in the structure of the church, and this at a time when in the civil area the role of the magistrates was consolidated and the will of the ruler was absolutized. In contrast to the Roman axiom, according to which an official was in principle irremovable during his term of office, the Christian congregations always preserved their freedom.[56] Obligated to their source, and thus to Christ as "priest forever" (Heb. 7:3), they sought to be just to their historical commission.[57]

VI

PARTICIPATION OF THE LAITY
IN CHURCH LEADERSHIP
AND IN CHURCH ELECTIONS

by

Hans Küng

The theme to be treated here is, surprisingly, not to be found in the Vatican II Decree on the Apostolate of the Laity. That fact makes the matter difficult. Participation, cooperation, collaboration of the laity in the decisions of the church? People like to talk of the participation of the laity in the *life* (not the decisions) of the church. They also like to speak of the participation of the laity in the decisions of the *world* (but not of the church). They do not at all like to speak, at least in official binding documents, of the participation of the laity in the *decisions* of the *church*. Nevertheless it is precisely here that the question of the status of the laity in the church arises in the most practical way. For as long as I can contribute advice and work, but am excluded from decision-making, I remain, no matter how many fine things are said about my status, a second-class member of this community: I am more an object that is utilized than a subject who is actively responsible. The person who can advise and collaborate, but not participate in decision-making in a manner befitting his status, *is* not really the church, but only *belongs to* the church. Yet this idea contradicts the very understanding of "laity" as we have once again seen it in the past decades, not least in Vatican II itself. It is not necessary here to go into the problematic of the somewhat unfortunate term "laity"; we not infrequently compensate for it by the use of such terms as "church" or "congregation," in contrast to the "shepherds" (presiding officers) or the "pastoral offices" (the supervisory offices).

Unfortunately the Decree on the Apostolate of the Laity of Vatican II, which carries on in a very long-winded and paternal fashion on various subjects that are quite obvious, remains on this point, which is so decisive in practical life, far behind what Yves Congar had already pioneered with concrete possibilities in the difficult preconciliar days by his courageous and epoch-making *Jalons pour une théologie du laïcat*.[1] Did this happen solely because this Decree on the Apostolate of the Laity came about without the active participation of the laity itself in the decision-making, and thus is essentially a product of clerics? Well, even Yves Congar is not a layman, but a cleric. That the decree has here a blind spot should be ascribed not so much to the clergy as clergy as to the clericalism of the clergy, a trait that can also be found among the laity.

The basis for joint decision in the church was itself laid out thoroughly in the decree, inasmuch as in the first section of the first preparatory chapter it was said that the laity "share in the priestly, prophetic, and royal office of Christ" and that from thence they "have their own role to play in the mission of the whole People of God in the Church and in the world" (Art. 2). And at the same time the decree alludes to the pertinent section of the Constitution on the Church, which will be reproduced here in full, because it explains in a concise, beautiful, and constructive way the basis on which our later reflections are grounded:

Therefore, the chosen People of God is one: "one Lord, one faith, one baptism" (Eph. 4:5). As members, they share a common dignity from their rebirth in Christ. They have the same filial grace and the same vocation to perfection. They possess in common one salvation, one hope, and one undivided charity. Hence, there is in Christ and in the Church no inequality on the basis of race or nationality, social condition or sex, because "there is neither Jew nor Greek; there is neither slave nor freeman; there is neither male nor female. For you are all 'one' in Christ Jesus" (Gal. 3:28; cf. Col. 3:11).

If therefore everyone in the Church does not proceed by the same path, nevertheless all are called to sanctity and have received an equal privilege of faith through the justice of God (cf. 2 Pet. 1:1). And if by the will of Christ some are made teachers, dispensers of mysteries, and shepherds on behalf of others, yet all share a true equality with regard to the dignity and to the activity common to all the faithful for the building up of the Body of Christ.

For the distinction which the Lord made between sacred ministers and the rest of the People of God entails a unifying purpose, since pastors and the other faithful are bound to each other by a mutual need. Pastors of the Church, following the example of the Lord, should minister to one another and to the other faithful. The faithful in their turn should enthusiastically lend their cooperative assistance to their pastors and teachers. Thus in their diversity all bear witness to the admirable unity of the Body of Christ. This very diversity of graces, ministries, and works gathers the children of God into one, because "all these things are the work of one and the same Spirit" (1 Cor. 12:11).[2]

Now if this is all true—and it is true—then the question arises spontaneously: If the community of all those in the church goes so deep in spite of all differences of gifts and services that it is not possible to go deeper, then why, considering the communality of the one Lord, of the one Spirit and the one Body, of one faith and one baptism, of one grace and vocation, of one hope and love, and finally of one responsibility and task—why then, despite all the diversity of functions is there not also in the church a communality of *decision?* On this one point the Constitution on the Church as well as the Decree on the Apostolate of the Laity remains timid. The medieval and post-Tridentine past still casts its long, heavy shadows upon them. It was in fact seen as great progress that the laity, who since Trent, or actually only since Vatican I, had been excluded from the councils, were again admitted at least in trifling numbers as auditors (the listening church!). Vatican I was a council of the pope, Vatican II a council of the bishops (and the theologians); as such they were great councils. But only Vatican III, it remains to hope, will be a council of priests and laity. The bishops fought courageously for collegiality: but only on the level of the universal church over against papal absolutism (papalism), and not on the level of the diocese over against its own similarly entrenched episcopal absolutism (episcopalism). Here is the task of the future, which some bishops already perceive! The Constitution on the Church (especially Arts. 33–38)—and very much less clearly the Decree on the Laity (especially Arts. 10, 20, 23–26), which was also decided upon by the hierarchy—speaks of course at great length and often still in an extremely paternalistic manner (with "fatherly love" the laity are addressed as the extensions and representatives of the clergy) of the much desired activity and collaboration of the laity, of involvement and encouragement, recognition and the fostering of the laity, of the usefulness of their advice and their experience. How laboriously and repeatedly the "concessions" to the laity had to be wrung almost word by word from the traditionalistic curial group for the Decree on the Laity as well as for the chapter on the laity of the Constitution on the Church is impressively shown by the excellent commentary by Ferdinand Klostermann.[3]

There is also repeatedly in the documents talk of possible agencies or lay councils (e.g., Constitution on the Church, Art. 37; Decree on the Apostolate of the Laity, Art. 26), which, however, according to the assertions of the documents, seem to have no more than an advisory function. The following passage from the Constitution on the Church is typical of the great openness and at the same time the time-bound narrowness of Vatican II:

> Let sacred pastors recognize and promote the dignity as well as the responsibility of the layman in the Church. Let them willingly make use of his prudent advice. Let them confidently assign duties to him in the service of the Church, allowing him freedom and room for action. Further, let them encourage the layman so that he may undertake tasks on his own initiative. Attentively in Christ, let them consider with fatherly love the projects, suggestions, and desires proposed by the laity. Furthermore, let pastors respectfully acknowledge that just freedom which belongs to everyone in this earthly city.

> A great many benefits are to be hoped for from this familiar dialogue between the laity and their pastors: in the laity, a strengthened sense of personal responsibility, a renewed enthusiasm, a more ready application of their talents to the projects of their pastors. The latter, for their part, aided by the experience of the laity, can more clearly and more suitably come to the decisions regarding spiritual and temporal matters. In this way, the whole Church, strengthened by each one of its members, can more effectively fulfill its mission for the life of the world. (Art. 37.)

This passage says much that was never found before in this form in official documents, and to that extent there has been a breakthrough to a new communality and community in the church. But the passage is also steadfastly silent on the question that must not be avoided or overlooked: if the laity are to be included as advisers and collaborators, then why not also as decision-makers?

FUNDAMENTAL PRINCIPLES

But are there perhaps serious theological objections, and not merely a centuries-long tradition of clericalism in the Catholic Church, which do indeed favor the participation of the laity in advising and working, but not in decision-making in the church? Is this not perhaps a misunderstanding of the real essence of the church, which is grounded not on a free accord of a believing individual, but on the call by God in Christ? Has not an essential differentness—a differentness that does not admit a translation of the modern democratic model to the church—been overlooked? Has not the hierarchical character of the church, which is built upon the apostles and the apostolic succession of the office-bearers and thus excludes any democratization, been forgotten? These and similar serious considerations should be answered, and of course not simply from the conciliar decrees, which in their treatment of this question have remained superficial, but from the original Christian message, as it expressed itself and operated in the church or the churches of the original New Testament age. What was originally correct cannot later on be rejected as false in principle by those who call themselves followers.

1. If we may, to begin with, argue from a more sociological point of view: Some of those who today reject joint decision-making with the laity in the church earlier rejected on the same basis any serious participation of the laity through collaboration and advising in the church. And some of those who protest today against a democratization of the church and against any translation of secular sociological models to the church not too long ago accepted without reflection the secular sociological model of the monarchy for the church, and even in practice did nothing against the monarchization of the church. They found no contradiction to the brotherhood of the New Testament[4] in conducting themselves in practice as mon-

archs, for the most part bound in no way by a constitution, but for all practical purposes absolute monarchs: petty and sometimes even very great and mighty kings and lords in their parishes ("Monsignor," i.e., "My Lord"), dioceses ("Your Graces," "Excellencies," and "Eminences"), and in the universal church ("Summus Pontifex" and "King of Kings and Lord of Lords"). This is not to say anything against the past, but it is past! In some countries Catholics even in this century opposed in every way possible the introduction of democratic forms into secular society in the name of this "divinely established" monarchical hierarchy, and Leo XIII was actually disgracefully insulted by ultra-Catholics when he finally abandoned the scruples of the hierarchical church toward the democratic form of government. In a nutshell: The man who has nothing against the monarchization of the church can really not have anything of a decisive theological nature against the democratization of the church. Basically it is better even in the church to speak of a democracy (the entire holy People of God) than of the "hierocracy" (a holy caste). For while in the New Testament all worldly honorary titles are strictly shunned in connection with bearers of office, they are in fact given to the entire believing people, which is designated "a chosen race, a royal priesthood, a consecrated nation" (I Peter 2:9), and made "a line of kings and priests, to serve our God and to rule the world" (Rev. 5:10).

But that already demonstrates that in decisive matters we are careful to argue not in sociological but in theological categories. Only in this way can we show that joint decision-making and regulation on the part of the laity not only is a timely concession to modern democratic developments, but is a move thoroughly rooted in the church's own origins. This is not to deny that the modern democratic development has not ultimately helped the church break out of her traditionalistic clerical encrustations and reflect on her original structure. Here a comparison with the democratic state can be helpful: As the citizens not only belong to the state, but in a full sense *are* the state, so all church members in a full sense are the church; they are all not mere inhabitants but full citizens of the church. Instead of this, the traditional concept of the church with its two-class theory, especially as it has operated since the Constantinian era in the entire ecclesiastical area, and after the Gregorian reform in its ultraclerical form, has relied mostly on other models. Among these models were the monarchist state (more frequently of an imperial-absolute style): ruler and ruled, commander and obedient; or the family: adults and minors, fathers and children; or the school: teachers and pupils (listeners); or property: owners (masters) and nonowners (servants).[5]

But can it be that the essence of the church seen from a theological perspective necessarily demands two classes or ranks, especially as the Code of Canon Law in canon 107 orders that "by virtue of divine institution" the clerics are to be differentiated from the laity in the church? [6] A further clarification is necessary.

2. Out of a correct—that is to say, Biblical and historical—perspective of "apostolic successions" there arises the question of the joint role of the laity in the decision-making in the church.[7] Here this can be indicated only briefly.[8] The special and unquestionable apostolic succession of the multiple pastoral service (the bishops with the pope, but in their way also the pastors with their co-workers) must not be isolated, but must be seen in its functionality:

a. The church *as a whole* (*Credo Ecclesiam apostolicam!*), and thus each individual church member, also stands in succession to the apostles. In what sense? The church, as well as all individuals, remains bound to the basic witness and service of the original witnesses without which there would be no church. The church is founded on the apostles (and the prophets). All the faithful thus are supposed to succeed the apostles in apostolic faith and confession, life and service. This service takes the most diverse forms of proclamation, baptism, the community of prayer and the Supper, the building up of the congregation, and service to the world.

b. The special apostolic succession of the diverse *pastoral service*, important as it is, is not thereby an end in itself. The pastoral service continues the special task of the apostles, in which they differentiate from other important and likewise permanent services in the church, such as that of the prophets or the teachers: namely, to establish and guide the churches. From this service of guiding the church, these office-bearers (bishops, pastors, further co-workers) also have a special authority; only in service can their authority have any foundation at all. The shepherds in the church are thus in no way a management class with a unilateral imperial power, toward which the single possible attitude is unilateral obedience. They are no *dominium,* but a *ministerium.* They form no power structure but a special service structure. "You know that among the pagans their so-called rulers lord it over them, and their great men make their authority felt. This is not to happen among you. No; anyone who wants to become great among you must be your servant, and anyone who wants to be first among you must be slave to all. For the Son of Man himself did not come to be served but to serve, and to give his life as a ransom for many." (Mark 10:42–45.)

So the purpose of shepherds in the church is special service to the apostolic church which is made up of all the believers. For this reason the term "hierarchy" or "holy rule" (customary only since the time of Dionysius the Pseudo-Areopagite five hundred years after Christ) is misleading. To be relevant Biblically, it is better to speak of *diakonia,* or "church service."

For the nurturing and constant growth of the People of God, Christ the Lord instituted in His Church a variety of ministries, which work for the good of the whole body. For those ministers who are endowed with sacred power are servants of their brethren, so that all who are of the People of God, and therefore enjoy a true Christian dignity, can work toward a common goal freely and in an orderly way, and arrive at salvation. (Constitution on the Church, Art. 18.)

Thus, if from a Biblical perspective the shepherds are not the masters but the servants of the church or the congregation (= the laity), why then should it in practice be possible to exclude the church or the congregation (= the laity) from joint decision-making? This can happen only if the shepherds are seen not as the servants of the church but as its exclusive owners or fathers or teachers.

But the shepherds are *not* the *owners* of the church, toward whom laity are only dependents who have nothing to say in the management. The church is not a huge industry: all members of the church *are* church; the church belongs to all of them. And the shepherds are also *not* the *fathers* of the church, in contrast to whom the laity are only minors who still cannot have any responsibility of their own for the church. The church cannot be considered simply as a family (except as under God, the one Father): all grown-up members of the church are adult members who have an established inalienable responsiblity for the whole. And, finally, the shepherds are also *not* the *teachers* of the church, in contrast to whom the laity are only learning pupils who have only to listen and to obey. The church is not a school: all church members have "learnt from God" (I Thess. 4:9) and "do not need anyone to teach" them (I John 2:27).

In brief: in the church, despite all the variations of office, which we must return to, all are ultimately equal insofar as they all are believers and, as such, adult brothers and sisters under the one Father and the one Lord Jesus. Teaching and advising, like listening and obeying, are, because all members are filled by the Spirit, *reciprocal*. To this extent the church, despite all differences of services, is no two-class society of possessor and nonpossessor, empowered and powerless, adults and minors, knowledgeable and ignorant, but a community of love filled and authorized by the Spirit in which only greater service bestows greater authority.

3. If then within this community of basic equality the variety of services and the special fullness of power of the pastoral office are nevertheless to be taken seriously, the question of the relation of the church (the local church or parish, the diocesan church, the universal church) to the relevant pastoral office (pastor and his co-workers, bishop, pope) must be defined anew: does the universal fullness of power of the church confirm the particular fullness of power of the pastoral office or is it the other way around —does the particular fullness of power of the pastoral office confirm the universal fullness of power of the church? This must be examined carefully.

a. The joint decision-making of the laity in the church can obviously *not be founded* on the fact that the fullness of power of the shepherds is derived simply from the fullness of power of the church or congregation, from the fullness of power of the universal priesthood. Then the special pastoral office would simply be leveled within the church and within the universal priesthood: an unbiblical democratization!

b. But, on the other hand, the participation of the laity in the decision-making of the church can also *not* be *excluded* on the basis that the fullness of power of the church or congregation is simply derived from the fullness of power of the shepherd, as though the shepherds alone stood in succession to the apostles and were not the servants of the church but its masters or mediators. Thus the pastoral service would be isolated from the church or congregation, from the universal priesthood, and its apostolic succession would be absolutized: an unbiblical hierarchicalization or clericalization of the church!

c. If, however, as we saw, the church and her shepherds stand all together under the one Father and Lord, who makes them all brothers, if they all stand under the one message of Christ and all are called into the same discipleship and the same obedience to God and his Word; if they then ultimately all are the hearing church and precisely as hearers are all filled with the Spirit, then it follows that the fullness of power of the church or congregation is not derived from the fullness of power of the shepherds, and the fullness of power of the shepherds is not derived from the fullness of power of the church or congregation, but the fullness of power of *both* is directly derived from the fullness of power of the Lord of the church in his Spirit. This common origin of their fullness of power establishes the universal authorization of the congregation as well as the special fullness of power of the service of the shepherds. It is the support of the authority of the shepherds as well as of the participation of the laity in decision-making.

4. The joint decision-making of the laity in the church will, then, be seen correctly only if church or congregation and the shepherds are seen as intimately related as well as different. It is this perspective which eliminates all absolutistic decision-making by either the shepherds *or* the congregation alone, which excludes both ecclesiastical oligarchy (monarchy) *and* ochlocracy. If, as we have emphasized, the universal priesthood, if the various charismatic gifts and offices, and if especially the charismata of the prophets and teachers are taken seriously in the church, then the *special office of the shepherds* (presiding officers) in the church must and will also be taken very seriously: it is the special vocation of individual believing persons (in principle—for there is no Biblical or dogmatic objection to it—both men and women) to the permanent and regular (not only occasional), public (not only private) service to the congregation as such (and not only to individual members) through the laying on of hands or

ordination (and not only through the equally possible charisma of the Spirit breaking through as He wills).

From this *special* service the shepherds have also *special* authority that can never be simply eliminated or passed over in the church or congregation. From this special *service,* however, they have their authority only within, for, and in collaboration with the church or congregation. So the *shepherds from the very outset are oriented to the joint collaboration, decision-making, and regulating of the congregation.* This orientation does not mean a constraint and restriction, but a protection against all stifling isolation, a help in all their need, a liberation into true togetherness. The shepherds must see their special fullness of power embedded and protected in the universal authorization of the church and of each individual church member. Solitary responsibility stifles, common responsibility sustains.

The Word, Baptism, the Eucharist, forgiveness, the office of love, are given to the entire church. But a few must discharge the service of the Word, the Sacrament, and the church permanently, regularly, and publicly in the church, strengthened and legitimized for this through prayer and the power of ordination, which itself should occur in cooperation with the entire church. Concretely: *all* Christians are empowered to preach the Word and to witness to the faith in the church and in the world; but only to the shepherds of the congregation who are called, or to those delegated by them, is the special fullness of power to preach in the congregational assembly given. *All* Christians are empowered to exhort men to forgive their brother in a crisis of conscience; but only to the called shepherds is given the special fullness of power of the words of reconciliation and absolution, which is exercised in the congregational assembly upon the congregation and thus upon the individuals. For the coexecution of Baptism and the Eucharist *all* Christians are authorized; but only to the called shepherds is given the special fullness of power to perform baptisms in public in the congregation and to conduct responsibly the congregational Eucharist.

5. Thus of their innermost essence the church or congregation and the shepherds are oriented toward one another in decision-making. On the basis of his special mission with which he steps before the congregation, the ordained shepherd has a pre-given authority in the church or the congregation. On the basis of his ordination the shepherd need not demonstrate his vocation, like every other charismatic, by the exhibition of his charisma (in proof of the Spirit and the power). Rather, he is appointed from the very beginning: legitimized as the one who is fully authorized for this office in a special way for the public activity of the congregation in the Spirit. But this must not be misunderstood, as though the shepherd ultimately were raised over the congregation to become the lord of the congregation, where he no longer remained dependent on the congregation. Every time a shepherd plays up his own person, every time he thinks and acts autocratically, conducts himself tyranically and autonomously, he betrays the mission that he has received. He is not understanding that his special mission is a charisma, a call from the Spirit, to gain which he can do nothing, which has been given him without his earning it. He is wandering astray from the gospel which he has been called to serve and which demands of him that he serve men. All this would be an error and a fault in him, and the congregation and each Christian would be justified and called upon by the Spirit to show his opposition through open witness, provided he acted in truth and love. If, however, the special mission of the shepherd is received in faith, embraced each day with new fidelity, and exercised in love, then it must also give to the man sent the certainty that he has been truly sent with authority, the confidence that he can measure up to the call despite all personal weakness, the courage to attack the task anew again and again and to proclaim the

word of God whether it is opportune or inopportune, the inner calm, despite all temptations, to endure to the end all crises and all assaults: "That is why I am reminding you now to fan into a flame the gift (charisma) that God gave you when I laid my hands on you. God's gift was not a spirit of timidity, but the Spirit of power, and love, and self-control. So you are never to be ashamed of witnessing to the Lord . . ." (II Tim. 1:6–8).

So the shepherd and the congregation have their mutual obligations: the shepherd has the duty and the task to proclaim the Christian message to the congregation again and again, even when it is uncomfortable for the congregation. The congregation, on the other hand, has the duty and the task of retesting again and again whether the shepherd is remaining true to his commission, whether he is acting according to the gospel. For there are not only false prophets, but also faithless shepherds. And if the Pauline statement "never try to suppress the Spirit or treat the gift of prophecy with contempt" (I Thess. 5:19 f.) holds true especially for the presiding officers, then what follows certainly holds true not only for some presiding officers, but for the entire congregation and each individual— "Think before you do anything—hold on to what is good and avoid every form of evil" (I Thess. 5:21 f.).

Thus everyone is helped by this mutual respectful examination, this reciprocal criticism without disputation, this universal *correctio fraterna* in modesty. And all this is a presupposition for common action, for which all that we have said is basically true: no individual decisions, neither of the church or congregation nor of the shepherd! No going-it-alone, neither of the laity without the shepherd nor of the shepherd without the laity. No sole control, neither dictatorship of the one nor dictatorship of the many! Instead of seclusion and isolation, openness and solidarity. Instead of paternalism, brotherliness. Instead of autocracy and despotism, service and love. Instead of servitude, freedom; instead of egotistic power, existence for others.[9]

6. If common responsibility, if joint decision-making of the congregation with the shepherd is seen in this way, then one need have no anxiety for the order of the congregation, even if it is threatened again and again from all sides. Then a first principle will be true for the shepherd as well as for the members of the congregation: to each his own! Then the shepherd will not assume a superiority over the congregation nor the congregation over the shepherd. Then neither shepherd nor laity will wish to commandeer and subordinate everything for themselves, but they will each give and relinquish what belongs to the other. And then a second principle is valid: *with one another for one another!* Then neither the shepherd nor the laity will use their fullness of power as a weapon against the other in order to grasp a position for themselves and seize the power in the church, but they will use this fullness of power, in the only way it makes sense, to serve one another and the whole. And finally there is one supreme criterion: *obedience to the Lord!* Then neither the shepherd nor the laity will play the role of Lord of the church, but find true freedom, imperturbable peace, and a permanent joy even amid difficulties and affliction in subordination to the one Lord and his Word in love.

In this way a correct perspective on *obedience* in the church is also possible. For Paul, the service that is actually occurring is the reason why subordination to those who make great exertions is obligatory. He who always volunteers for a special service—not only that of the shepherd, but also of the prophet or teacher or helper, etc. —and proves himself in it, he has the call of God, he has received the gift of grace of the Spirit. It is not simply a certain station, not a special tradition, not great age, not a long membership in the congregation, not even finally a conferring of the Spirit, but service itself perfected in the Spirit which creates authority in the congregation. Thus the obedience of everyone to God, Christ, the Spirit, is demanded: here *unconditional* obedience is valid. But toward men, whose will after all is certainly not always in accord with the will of God, there is even in the church only a *conditional* and never a unilateral obedience. Free reciprocal subordination, free service of all for all, free obedience toward the always-other gifts of grace of the other, is the consequence of obedience of all to God, Christ, the Spirit. The one Lord acts in one Spirit not only through the shepherds but through all the various gifts of grace (I Cor. 12:4–6). And the whole life of the church will thus be a united living ensemble of shepherds and congregation, including all the various spiritual gifts and offices, amid which order and peace should rule—and yet the Spirit must never be muffled.

EMBODIMENT

The embodiment of an ecclesiastical order that is justified by the original Christian message and church must be different for different times and different places. In every case a transposition is necessary. Thus it is far from our intention to deliver a hard, unhistorical judgment on times in which this ecclesiastical order was realized only very imperfectly.[10] And likewise it is not our intention to give a simple prescription for a universal remedy for a better realization of such a truly Christian order to all the varied areas of the church. Nevertheless, attention ought to be called to a few points of a general nature.

Precisely what are the concrete possibilities for the participation of the laity in the decision-making of the church? Yves Congar has called attention to the most important in the above-mentioned book:[11]

1. The role of the laity in elections, and the occupying of ecclesiastical offices.
2. The role of the laity in councils.
3. The role of the princes in the church.
4. The role of the congregation in the ordering of their own life through the law of use and custom.

5. The participation of the laity in the administration of church property and in ecclesiastical jurisdiction.

The role of the laity in the Council we have treated in detail on another occasion.[12] In view of the contemporary postconciliar situation, continuing Congar's thought and at the same time following certain items in the Council documents themselves, we can mention two ways in which the participation of the laity in decision-making can be concretized: first in the collegial church leadership on the various levels and then also in the free election of presiding officers through a representation of the pertinent churches.[13]

1. *The collegial church leadership on the various levels.* The "collegiality" emphasized by the Council, that is, the brotherly-communal character of church leadership, must not arbitrarily remain limited to the uppermost level of the universal church (pope—bishops). It must also be realized on the level of the national church, the diocesan church, and above all the local church (and correspondingly also in the religious orders with their lay brothers). That means very clearly a dissolution of that authoritarian one-man rule—whether on the level of the parish, bishopric, nation, or the universal church—which, as we have seen, is consonant neither with the original New Testament organization nor with contemporary democratic thought.

According to what we have already said about the shepherds, it is quite clear that the decisive authority of the pastor, the bishop, and the pope should remain explicitly preserved; only in this way can the mutual paralysis of the various powers normally be avoided. Nevertheless at the same time not only collaboration and counseling but also participation in decision-making by representative councils of the churches in question should be guaranteed. In order that these councils be truly representative it is necessary that the greater part of the members be elected in free and secret elections; a minority can be members ex officio because of certain important service functions or through their nomination by responsible shepherds (pastor, bishop, bishops' conference, or pope).

The constitutional foundations for these pressing and incisive reforms are laid down, at least for the diocese, by the Council itself: it was resolved by Vatican II that in every diocese a diocesan pastoral council should be established, to be composed of priests, religious, and laity. This pastoral council is already a reality in some dioceses, wherein the priests' council, also decreed by the Council, is partly integrated into this pastoral council, and the laity often have a two-thirds majority. In the concrete statutes of the diocesan council, care must be taken to assure that a true participation in decision-making is guaranteed, in which a kind of veto power (or a necessity of agreement) can be vested in the authorized shepherd. An appearance of collegiality, which admits no true participation of the council in decision-making, can do more harm than good; it is nothing but the collegial cloak for the old princely absolutism. Thus—a warning example to other levels—it was depressing to see how already at the first episcopal synod in Rome after the Council, true collegiality was completely overruled by the old papal absolutism: the things to be settled were unilaterally established and narrowed by the curial side, the most pressing problems of the universal church (like regulation of births and celibacy) could not be discussed, no experts were admitted, much was discussed and resolved, but nothing was decided; the bishops traveled home without knowing which of these agreements the pope and the curial apparatus would bring to realization; practically speaking, the bishops' synod had no serious immediate effects.

Analogous to the diocesan level, collegial leadership of the church must also be realized on the other levels:

a. For the universal church it would mean to constitute a lay council parallel to the bishops' council which is already constituted, though still not permanent, still not assembling regularly, and still possessing no authority. This could come about as a result of the international lay congress, which in the postconciliar period showed more vitality, courage, and resolution than the synod of bishops. This lay council, together with the bishops' council under the decisive leadership of the pope (the veto power), could not only give advice but also decide on the important concerns of the universal church.

b. For each nation there should be constituted, again paralleling the diocesan pastoral council, a national pastoral council, consisting of bishops, priests, and laity, for counseling and communal decision-making in all important concerns of the national church.

c. For every parish there should be constituted, where this has not already happened, a parish council of men and women, paralleling the diocesan pastoral council, for the purposes of counseling and participation in decision-making with the pastor (who would have veto power) in all important parish concerns.

For the concrete statute the following should be observed:

a. In all the decision-making councils we have described, from the parish council to the lay senate and the bishops' council of the entire church, it should be self-explanatory that a sufficient number of qualified *women* are also to be admitted as members. Such representation is a part of the full participation of women in the life of the church on the basis of equality. On the various levels care must be taken eventually for the education and inclusion of women in active co-responsibility.

b. On every level, theological and other *professional people* are to be drawn in, corresponding to the scholarly areas under discussion.

c. For practical functioning, the American principle of "checks and balances," which precludes a monopolization of power in certain hands, is helpful. In the United States the president as well as Congress has a strong post. And so ultimately the president can do nothing without Congress, and Congress can do nothing without the president. The executive branch (the president) can employ a strong initiative and in emergency even a strong brake. But it is bound by the resolutions of the legislative branch (Congress), against which the president can—but in practice seldom does—apply a veto. Moreover, both the president and Congress are controlled by the judiciary branch (the courts). So the president and Congress mutually hinder and help one another. Autocracy and the dictatorship of an individual is avoided, just as is ochlocracy and the fragmentation of the many, all of which benefits both the freedom of the individual and the well-being of the whole.[14]

2. *Free election of presiding officers by a representation of the pertinent churches.* This should hold true for pastors, bishops, and pope. Such an election can be arranged with the cooperation of the representative councils discussed above, to which, circumstances permitting, other members can be co-opted for the electoral college: for the election of the pope in the universal church, the bishops' council and lay council would be duly qualified; for the election of the bishop in the diocese, the diocesan pastoral council; for the election of the pastor in the local church, the parish council (or as in some Swiss cantons, the assembled congregation).

In the election of the pastor and bishops a control function would belong to the superior pastoral offices: the election of pastors would have to be approved by the bishops, the election of bishops by the episcopal conference in its majority or by the pope. In this way the old axioms of canon law would once again hold good and could be applied by analogy to all ecclesiastical offices: "No bishop should be installed against the will of the people" (Pope Celestine I) and "He who presides over all should be elected by all" (Pope Leo the Great).

As to concrete regulations, several points would be important:

a. Election not only of the superiors of religious orders, or, as in certain church areas, the pastor, but also of the bishops and all officeholders for a substantial but stipulated time (e.g., six or eight years with the possibility of reelection) is a justified as well as a pressing desideratum in today's situation.

b. Directives for obligatory (e.g., at 70 years) or optional (e.g., at 65 years) resignation from ecclesiastical offices are necessary. On the other side, demands of a congregation for the retirement of a shepherd should never be legally binding without the agreement of the superior officeholder (bishop for the pastor, pope or episcopal conference for the bishop); in this way illegitimate attempts at pressure can be averted from the pertinent administrator.

c. A special committee should advise the bishop in all personnel concerns; such a group can consider each case carefully—the special peculiarities and requisites of the position concerned as well as the wishes of the congregation and of the person in question. Special attention must be given to the pastor-assistant relationship, which is full of vexation.

Only one example, though one which has central significance, shall be investigated here more closely: election of bishops.[15] The election of the bishop of Rome, the pope, will not be treated specially here; nevertheless it must be clear even without a long explanation how pressing the transferral of the election from the college of cardinals, which is in no way representative and in any case is anachronistic, to the episcopal and lay councils is: today more than ever the pope needs the broadest consensus in the church!

The election of the bishop by a representative council of the pertinent church satisfies the following:

1. the theological as well as practical high esteem for the particular and local church, for the diocese and the congregation (cf. esp. the Constitution on the Church, Art. 26, and the Constitution on the Bishops, e.g., Art. 27);

2. the demand for decentralization, which stipulates a dismantling of the power of the Roman Curia in favor of the churches in the individual nations (establishment of national bishops' conferences, etc.; cf. Decree on the Bishops, e.g., Arts. 36–38);

3. the demand for a curial reform (which, unfortunately, has still not been radically accomplished), which will provide not a broadening of the area of curial competence over against the episcopates of individual countries, but on the contrary the insertion of representatives of the most varied countries into the ecclesiastical central administration (cf. Constitution on the Bishops, Arts. 9–10);

4. the strict definition (which here would mean limitation) of the authority of the nuncio, as desired by the Council: "The Fathers also eagerly desire that, in view of the pastoral role proper to bishops, the office of legates of the Roman Pontiff be more precisely determined" (Decree on the Bishops' Pastoral Office in the Church, Art. 9; cf. Art. 10).

For a historical understanding of these conclusions of Vatican II it must be remembered that these conclusions doubtless stand in a clear front line against Roman centralism, dirigism, and absolutism, as it has prevailed in the West since the Gregorian reform and the High Middle Ages and reached its unsurpassable high point in the period after Vatican I with the new codification of the Code of Canon Law. But on the basis of what has been stated here from the New Testament, it must be clear that these conclusions are not concerned with attempted "innovations," but with a return to tradition,[16] the truly good old tradition. The election of bishops is itself an excellent model for this, as it was earlier. In the election of bishops it was from the beginning kept in mind that not only a clerical hierarchy of functionaries but rather the entire community of believers, the entire People of God, is the church. In ancient Christian times the bishop was *elected by clergy and people,* even if he then was ordained generally by the neighboring bishops. Some of the greatest bishops of all times, such as Ambrose of Milan and Augustine of Hippo, were elected decisively by the people. *Nos eligimus eum,* "We elect him," ran the formula of acclamation of the people in the Latin congregations. Not the Roman bishop but the neighboring bishops authoritatively cooperated in the election. The right of corroboration and consecration also belonged later, according to the stipulations of the First Ecumenical Council of Nicaea, not to the Roman see but to the metropolitan of the ecclesiastical province involved. How the nomination to the episcopal sees passed in later times in part to the princes, and how the Biblically based right of the people of the church was more and more limited cannot be treated here in detail. In any case the reform movement of the Middle Ages still demanded the free election of bishops by clergy and people (so decreed Leo IX at the Synod of Rheims in 1049). The free episcopal election as over against nomination by the princes succeeded in principle in the battle over investiture. Indeed, because of the growing predominance of the cathedral chapter, the lower clergy and the laity were more and more excluded from the election. At first the cathedral chapter had only to assent to an election, then more and more it could determine the election. The election right of the cathedral chapter became common toward the end of the twelfth century and was established as obligatory by Innocent III for the entire church.

Through this development, favored by the popes, the right of corroboration and ordination more and more fell to the Roman see, although in the early centuries the influence of the Roman bishop in reference to episcopal elections did not extend essentially beyond his metropolitan (or patriarchal) right, and only after the ninth century in case of complications (removal, promotion, election controversies) did he regularly interfere in the filling of a vacancy. After the High Middle Ages the right of corroboration was often used for the purpose of exerting influence on the election itself. This eventuated in the reservations by which the popes withheld to themselves the filling of episcopal seats: first of all for isolated cases, then for certain seats, finally after the fourteenth century (under the Avignon Pope Urban V, in 1363) in general. Thus the suffrage of the chapter was undermined and in time even legally suppressed. Only after the Western Schism and in the struggle over the Council of Basel was an at least circumscribed episcopal suffrage of the cathedral chapter again recognized through the Viennese Concordat of 1448. Indeed, it came about in the aftermath of the development of a royal or noble right of nomination which took many forms (in some cases the right of lesser acceptibility: *personae minus gratae*). With the abolition of the Catholic ruling houses these rights declined vastly. In this manner the way was first cleared for a general papal naming of bishops, which had already long been in the making and now was established in proper form in the new *Codex Iuris Canonici,* which was proclaimed by Rome in 1918 without any essential participation of the episcopacy and amid the complete exclusion of the universal church. The chiefly unrestricted rights to elect bishops in the Swiss bishoprics of Basel, Chur, and St. Gall, as well as of Olmütz, remain now the great exceptions. Only in the Eastern churches united to Rome has the right of nomination formed in the ancient church era to an extent remained preserved, and the new law of the Eastern churches recently accepted the rule that the bishop be elected by the synod of bishops of the patriarchs. Yet this freedom of election is diluted insofar as the list of candidates must be approved by Rome in advance! The spirit of the resolutions of Vatican II means a reinclusion of clergy and laity in the election of bishops after the model of the ancient church.[17]

In conclusion let us say only this: Obviously there is no perfect system of organization; in concrete life, each has its specific defects and dangers. But a system better than that canonized by the present Code of Canon Law is not difficult to think of! The one suggested here in some of its basic features corresponds better both to the original organization of the apostolic church and to our contemporary democratic times.

VII

PEOPLE, PRIESTS, AND BISHOPS IN U.S. CATHOLIC HISTORY
by
Leonard Swidler

In many ways there is a striking parallel between the developments of the Catholic Church during the nineteenth century in America and Europe, particularly Germany. In the beginning of that century there was a certain amount of turmoil and at the same time a concern for freedom within the church. In Europe this was manifested in the growth of the influence of the Enlightenment, or *Aufklärung,* as the Germans called it, within Catholicism. This influence probably had its most beneficial effects in German Catholicism, where a kind of Vatican II Catholicism flourished 150 years before that Council; the renewal of *Aufklärung* Catholicism was very broad, covering lithurgical reform, a Biblical movement, catechetical renewal, ecumenism, stress on the laity, emphasis on individual liberty and freedom of conscience, and the need for decentralizing and democratizing the structures of the church. Then came the long decades during the middle portion of the century when reaction gained dominance, culminating in Vatican I; the gains for freedom in the earlier part of the century were wiped out; extreme centralizing and authoritarian measures were taken. The last two decades of the century witnessed a notable renewal in Catholic thought and life, particularly in the attitude toward modern methods and developments, ranging from the "democratizing priests" and what was later dubbed "modernism" in France, through *Reformkatholizismus* in Germany, to *Rinnovamento* in Italy. But all this was cut short by the blight of the antimodernist heresy-hunt just before World War I, the effects of which lasted and in many ways remained dominant until after World War II, and were really displaced only by the hard-fought battles of Vatican II.

This new nation came into existence just before the beginning of the nineteenth century in the atmosphere of the Enlightenment and liberty. The American preoccupation with freedom was reflected in this period in the prominent place laymen took in the church and the relative independence from outside influences American Catholic Church leaders sought. As in Europe, this "freedom" period was followed by many decades throughout the middle part of the nineteenth century wherein the laymen's responsible role disappeared and centralized authoritarianism increased; lay trusteeism was crushed and the bishop became more and more "the pope" in his own diocese. Then for almost the last two decades of the century an extraordinary renewal occurred, including a "lay renaissance" and a going out to meet the contemporary world on its own terms by church leaders—a movement referred to generally as Americanism.[1] But this renewal too was aborted by the condemnation of the "heresy of Americanism" just before the end of the century, and American Catholicism tended to become super-ultramontane, defensive, and sterile, until Pope John threw open the window of Vatican II.

LAY TRUSTEEISM

To return to the beginning of United States history: the freedom and responsibility of the various elements of the Catholic Church in America were zealously promoted. The laity had a serious role in the appointment of their pastors and in church affairs; the clergy of America elected one of their number for their first bishop; the American episcopacy immediately thereafter had a major influence in subsequent appointments of bishops. However, by the second quarter of the nineteenth century, the freedom and the responsibility of each of these three elements were being drastically restricted—what the bishops lost in power to Rome was more than compensated for by what they took for themselves from the other two groups, the priests and the people. Virtually only two bishops, John Carroll (bishop of Baltimore, 1789–1815) and John England (bishop of Charleston, 1820–1842), in this period—indeed, until the last decades of the nineteenth century—strove for a more balanced distribution of freedom and responsibility, but to no lasting avail.

One of the first issues of major concern the student of Catholic history in the United States comes up against is lay trusteeism. If priests recalled only one thing from their seminary study of American church history, it was, at least until recently, doubtless the story of how laymen, trustees, attempted to seize unwarranted power in the church and only with great effort were put back in their place. Many, if not most, priests ordained before Vatican II have not infrequently recalled the evils of trusteeism as a caution against any movement to place responsibility—other than that of making donations—in the hands of laymen. Yet, despite the great breadth of superficial knowledge about trusteeism, there is no thorough study of the phenomenon.[2] Portions of the story are found in snatches in such large works as *The Life and Times of*

John Carroll, and *The Life and Times of John England,*
by Msgr. Peter Guilday, published in the 1920's, and also
in the local histories of certain parish churches and dioceses. There is also a tiny handful of articles dealing with
"The Evils of Trusteeism," "Trusteeism in the Atlantic
States, 1785–1863," [3] and the like. But these articles are
often either very summary or clerically tendentious. In
fact, there is a bit of irony in the article on trusteeism
by the outstanding American Catholic Church historian
Peter Guilday. It is entitled simply "Trusteeism," [4] and
runs to sixty-four printed pages, but in it almost no evidence of recalcitrance or intrigue by the lay trustees is
offered. However, a great deal of evidence of intrigue
among priests, bishops, and Roman ecclesiastics is brought
forth—covering about 95 percent of the article. Likewise, a reading of the material that is available outside
of archives immediately makes one suspicious about the
accuracy of the picture drawn. Trusteeism is usually
spoken of as an "evil" and such phrases as "afflicted the
American Church" [5] are often used in connection with it.
Some of the things referred to with abhorrence by these
historians seem today quite acceptable. But that is perhaps not surprising, for these men were mostly clerics
writing in an age during which clericalism was dominant
in American Catholicism. The assumption is inevitably
made by these Catholic Church historians that the bishop
was always right and the layman wrong. How total the
identification of the church with hierarchy was is indicated in even the language of the magisterial Msgr. Peter
Guilday: "This rebellion is known in American Catholic
annals as the Trustee System. The right to administer ecclesiastical property belongs to the *Church* [italics added].
This right can be delegated to others, cleric or lay, as
accessory administrators responsible to her for their management of such property. [Clearly when Guilday says
"Church" he, perhaps unconsciously, means bishops, else
how could the right be delegated to *others?* His next word

(following this comment), the third person plural posses-
sive pronoun, confirms this understanding.] *Their* [italics
added] deputies are known as *church wardens, sidesmen,
fabrica, fabrique de l'église,* or as *trustees.*" [6] But if the
full, more balanced story must await new basic historical
efforts, it is nevertheless essential that at least a partial
sketch of what happened be attempted here.

As Guilday pointed out, from very early in the history
of Christianity, church income was divided into three
parts, one for the support of the clergy, one for the poor,
and one for the upkeep of the church buildings and related matters, the latter being referred to as the fabric
of the church. Through the centuries those contributing
to this fund had varying degrees of responsibility for its
distribution. Guilday wrote: "This system was universal in
the Church down to the sixteenth century and was recognized by the Council of Trent. In almost all Catholic
countries today the old system of the *fabrique de l'église*
still prevails. From the time of the Reformation the
system died out among the Catholics of Great Britain
and Ireland and it has not been in general usage in these
countries since that time. In the United States, lay trustees
are found at the very beginning of the organized Church,
and the system of trustees has prevailed down to the
present; it has been recognized by the Plenary Councils,
particularly by the Third Plenary Council of Baltimore." [7]

The immediate reason why the trustee system was introduced into the American scene, even though it had
died out in England and Ireland, was very clearly outlined by a priest very much involved in one of the trustee
affairs early in the nineteenth century, Father William
Vincent Harold, O.P. In writing to Rome he stated:
"Each church is, by an act of the legislature of the state
in which it is situated, made a distinct corporation, and
this incorporated body possesses all the rights and privileges of a citizen of the States. . . . The income of the
churches is principally derived from an annual rent which

each member of the congregation pays for his seat (pew) in the church. . . . These pew rents and burial charges are recoverable by law. It was considered an odious and a dangerous thing for the priest to appear in a Court of Justice, as the prosecutor of his flock even for the recovery of just debts. Yet this would sometimes have been inevitable had he been appointed the legal representative of the church property. It was therefore thought prudent that a certain number of the respectable lay members of each church should be elected for these purposes. The Pastor is always President of the board, and no act of the trustees can have legal force without his signature. To prevent the abuse of power the lay trustees are annually elected. The priest is the only member whom the law recognizes as permanent without election." [8]

The difficulties with the trustee system in America usually arose over the appointment or dismissal of the pastor of a church. The picture often communicated in American Catholic Church history is that large numbers, indeed most, of the parishes in the first decades of this country's history were controlled by lay trustees who wished to have unrestrained power of appointment and dismissal.[9] This picture of course is a grave distortion of the facts even as we now know them. In the three quarters of a century of controversy over the trustee system there do not seem to have been much more than a dozen prominent trustee difficulties in all the United States. Besides this quantitative exaggeration there has often been a qualitative distortion by the assumption of most Catholic Church historians that the attitude and actions of the trustees were always wrong and those of the bishop right, that the trustees always claimed, or were about to claim, total power to appoint and dismiss pastors, and the bishops always only defended the essential rights of "the Church" (meaning the bishop) from usurpers. Again, the facts, even as they come through the present secondary literature (that is, when long quotations of documents are reproduced), point in a different direction, or rather, many different directions. The various trustee cases were not all of a piece, but often were quite different in many essential elements. The common elements were: (1) Most often the difficulties were started by a *priest* who somehow became involved in a dispute with either the congregation or the bishop; (2) the trustees then wanted to have some kind of voice in resolving the problem, which usually included some sort of role in the appointment, confirmation, or dismissal of the pastor; (3) the bishop attempted to solve the conflict by avoiding schism wherever possible, but always retaining his ultimate power of appointment, which power was sometimes shared, but, as time went on, was exercised more and more absolutely.

In the first years of the American Catholic Church "there was normally a bending over backwards to give the laity as much freedom as possible; to adapt, in the end, the American Church as much as possible to the American scene and the temperament of American Catholics. In this respect, Carroll was not just being practical. He was himself firmly committed to the American freedoms which he and his flock enjoyed with all other Americans." [10] Even before he was elected the first American Catholic bishop, while he was the American Prefect-apostolic, he wrote to Cardinal Antonelli in Rome: "We desire that the faith in its integrity, due obedience towards the Apostolic See and perfect union should flourish; and at the same time that whatever can with safety to religion be granted, shall be conceded to American Catholics in ecclesiastical affairs. In this way we hope that distrust of Protestants now full of suspicion will be diminished and that our affairs can be solidly established." [11]

The first trustee case that John Carroll encountered was at St. Peter's Church in New York, where in 1785 a dispute between the two priests serving it developed and the trustees eventually took one side and appealed to Carroll to support their position, namely, to appoint Father Nugent (the second priest to arrive in New York) as chaplain of their church. In a long letter dated January 25, 1786, Father Carroll carefully responded to the trustees, deploring any prospect of making clergymen totally dependent on the congregation (which was a good point to make even though that was not what was being attempted then—it is also always the point that is volubly referred to and quoted), and cautioning the trustees not to seek a solution to the conflict in the civil courts. However, in the same letter Carroll also basically sided with the trustees and appointed Father Nugent cochaplain— a fact that, of course, could not be glossed over but that is never made much of by Catholic Church historians. But what is of even more interest in that letter is Father Carroll's statement about the appointment of clergymen to parishes: "Wherever parishes are established no doubt, a proper regard (and such as is suitable to our governments) will be had to *rights of the congregation in the mode of election and representation.*" [12] This clear statement seems almost never to be alluded to, quoted, or commented on. In fact, on a number of occasions Carroll received requests from trustees of churches indicating that they had chosen a certain priest for their pastor and were asking his approval and appointment of him, with which request he often complied. In another letter to the trustees of Holy Trinity Church in Philadelphia, where another dispute had arisen over languages and nationalities, Father Carroll again referred to the election of the pastor by the congregation in an approving manner, as long as the appointment was not "without the concurrent of the ecclesiastical superior." He wrote: "Let the election of the pastor of your new church be so settled that every danger of a tumultuous appointment be avoided as much as possible." [13] This letter too, which is quoted only in piecemeal fashion by Monsignor Guilday, seems never to be commented on or quoted elsewhere.[14]

Unfortunately, neither Carroll's subsequent fellow bishops nor his successors had his concern for liberty or his ability—save John England, bishop of Charleston from 1820 to 1842. Carroll's second successor as archbishop of Baltimore, Ambrose Maréchal, in a report to Rome in 1818 [15] noted that Carroll had "defended" the trustee system, but that on the day before he died he supposedly told his coadjutor, Leonard Neale, that he regretted permitting the system—of course, we have no direct evidence that he said something like this, nor what sort of legitimate interpretation should be put on it within its context if it was said. In short: until contrary evidence is available, John Carroll's actions over many years speak louder than someone else's words about his words allegedly uttered the day before he died, in 1815, aged 80.

However, even Archbishop Maréchal, in the same report to Rome in 1818, spoke of a conception of the trustee system that retained for the laity a restricted but serious voice in the affairs of the local churches: "As far as I am concerned, it seems to me that it could be allowed without danger if the temporal administrators were restricted by means of certain clauses, either in the title of possession itself or in a contract, which they would be obliged to sign at the time of their election, so that they could not abuse the civil right entrusted to them; for example, that a pastor in his sacred functions be altogether independent of them; that if he be guilty or accused of some fault, the case be taken to the bishop and that he be considered innocent as long as the bishop has not condemned him; that they might never remove him from the church on their own private authority." [16]

Just four years later, in 1822, Maréchal received strong support for his relatively moderate position from Pope Pius VII. In a brief entitled *Non sine magno* Pius VII granted the rights of the trustees over the temporalities of the local churches so long as they did not attempt to exercise "immoderate and unlimited rights . . . independently of the diocesan Bishops," that is, appointing and dismissing pastors without the bishop's approval.[17] Unfortunately, however, Rome did a very poor job in providing episcopal leadership in the years after Carroll's death, and largely because of that a number of trustee disputes developed and lingered on. In 1829 the first Provincial Council of Baltimore took one step toward eliminating the trustee problem (by effectively eliminating the trustees) by ruling that wherever possible no church was to be erected without being legally assigned to the bishop.[18] Although the trustee system is acknowledged to have been a real benefit to the development of the church in the Midwest,[19] the system was from 1829 onward more and more effectively strangled by the bishops. As the century wore on, the bishops received a growing support for their authoritarian leadership from the ever-increasing floods of immigrants (mostly Irish during the first half of the nineteenth century) that poured into America. Because of their most often peasant European background, the Catholic immigrants tended to be conservative, submissive to the church, and suspicious of the state—the very opposite of German *Aufklärung* Catholics, who were dominant in many parts of Germany during the first third or more of the nineteenth century, and also the native American Catholics. But long before the Civil War the clerically oriented Irish immigrant Catholics dominated the church in America, providing authoritarian leaders such as Archbishop Hughes of New York with the mace to smash the remnants of an effective lay voice in the American church. The development of anti-Catholic nativism during this same period, of course, only drove the security-seeking people and the authoritarian clerical leaders closer together.[20]

JOHN ENGLAND THE CONSTITUTIONALIST

As suggested above, the spiritual successor to John Carroll was the Irishman John England, appointed the first bishop of Charleston, South Carolina, in 1820. England came into a so-called trustee situation that was on the verge of schism. He immediately redirected the energies of the persons and groups involved and completely dissipated the problem. He was a man of extraordinary intelligence, great oratorical ability, wide journalistic experience, winning affability, and enormous capacity for work. Immediately upon his arrival he set out upon a months-long, arduous tour of his diocese, both the Carolinas and Georgia, speaking to every known Catholic possible, instructing, organizing, and preaching almost incessantly—it is surprising to note back through the stereotypes of Southern anti-Catholic prejudice and hatred that Dr. England was besought everywhere throughout the South to stay and preach at length in Protestant churches, which he did. England very quickly discerned the American spirit and love of liberty and thereupon set about devising a constitution by which his diocese would be governed. Bishop England did not wish to, nor was he at liberty to, give up the substantial ruling powers of the local bishop. However, he also felt that priests and laity should have a significant voice in the affairs of the church, which he provided for by his constitution.

England's constitution met one of the central points contested in the trustee disputes head on: it stipulated that the right and power to appoint clergymen to ecclesiastical duties belonged to the bishop. But it also provided grievance machinery whereby the laity could seek redress from allegedly improper actions of their pastor, while still protecting the clergyman from a fickle or vindictive mob.[21] A general diocesan fund was set up, which was to be disposed of by the general convention. The convention was to meet every year[22] and was composed of three parts: the bishop; a house of clergy, made up of representatives of all the clergy of the area; and a house of laity, made up of representatives of all the laity on a proportional basis. "The problems met in these Conventions were practically the same on a smaller scale as those which have occupied the minds of our bishops in the United States since that time: Catholic education, elementary and secondary; seminary training and the formation of a national clergy; social welfare work among the laboring classes; the care of the poor, the ailing, and the immigrant; watchfulness over legislation during anti-Catholic movements; the defense of the Faith and of Catholic moral principles; the spread of Catholic literature, and the support of the Catholic Press." [23]

Although the constitution made it clear that the power of decision in strictly ecclesiastical matters resided in the bishop, it also stated that "The House of the Clergy has power to examine into the ecclesiastical concerns of such establishments and to make its private report thereon to the Bishop or Vicar, together with its opinion and advice." [24] England was keenly aware of the difficulties that could arise from the presence of headstrong priests but he was also conscious that their situation as a group in the United States left them open to arbitrary action by authoritarian bishops; he argued at Rome that "another grave cause of disorder is the absence of any legislation in the American Church for the protection of the priests. Having only delegated jurisdiction in their parishes *ad nutum episcopi,* they are at the mercy of a bishop's whims and fancies, and have no means of appeal from unjust censures or penal inflictions." [25] Unfortunately England's seems to have been almost a lone episcopal voice championing the cause of priests vis à vis their bishops in the rising tide of Catholic authoritarianism in the nineteenth century.

In the same report to Rome, England also argued both for supradiocesan councils and for including the lay voice in enacting church regulations, in the style of his own annual conventions; he contended that "the American people are a law-abiding people, and laws are respected so long as the voice of the people is had in its making. They will not obey whimsical legislation and to a certain extent, in the absence of Provincial Councils, ecclesiastical legislation is of that kind." [26] About the same time, in a letter from Rome he again expressed his desire for the development of conciliar and synodal elements in the governance of the church. He wrote: "Our opponents had their monthly, yearly and triennial meetings of Presbyteries, Synods, Assemblies, Conferences, Conventions and Societies, by means of which they had common counsel, unity of action, concentrated force, and powerful influence as well as of public respect, whilst they by adopting this catholic principle of ancient discipline were daily and yearly growing compact, soothing their jealousies and collecting large means which they applied to common objects after common consultation, we were a parcel of disunited congregations, having no common consultation, no unity of action, no rallying point, growing daily more jealous and more divided, and having no practical union." [27]

All of England's strengths—his intelligence, his liberality, his charm, his diligence, his oratorical ability, and most of all his success—were weaknesses with his fellow American bishops. Their main response to him was that of fear and envy. His constitution and the irritating fact that it obviously worked were the special objects of episcopal delations and denunciations to Rome.[28] Although England received a somewhat vague reprimand from the Roman office of the Propaganda de fide, under whose jurisdiction the American church was, he later received a specific apology from the then head of the Propaganda, Cardinal Cappellari,[29] who a few months later, in 1831, became Pope Gregory XVI; ironically it was the same Gregory XVI who in 1832 issued the notorious bull *Mirari vos,* in which he viciously attacked separation of church from state, freedom of the press, and freedom of conscience, referring to the latter as a "madness." [30] It should be noted that it was also during this same period, the 1820's and 1830's, that an extremely strong movement for synodal government developed within German Catholicism, but with no lasting success. It must also be reported that when Bishop England died in 1842, his constitution, though eminently successful, died with him—the convention never met again. Thus, in America, as in Europe, the swirling waters of rising reactionary Catholicism began to sweep away whatever libertarian gains had been made in the earlier part of the nineteenth century.

THE SELECTION OF BISHOPS

A similar historical pattern in the appointment of bishops also appears to have held true, beginning with liberal involvement of the American clergy in general in the selection of future bishops, proceeding to the total elimination of the voice of the priests as the century developed. On March 12, 1788, a clergy petition from representatives of the American priests was addressed to the pope asking that the first American Catholic bishop be appointed: "that the election of the bishop, at least for the first time, be permitted to the priests, who now duly exercise the religious ministry here and have the care of souls." [31] The response of the Holy See was favorable: "that His Holiness would grant that, *on the first occasion at least,* the bishop be nominated by that part of the clergy which at present has the care of souls in the said provinces." [32] In the immediate subsequent correspondence from Rome, the Holy See was at great pains to state several times that this right of the priests to elect their bishop was a special privilege: "And whereas by special grant, and for this time only, we have allowed the priests exercising the care of souls in the United States of America, to elect a person to be appointed Bishop by us, and almost all their votes have been given to our beloved Son, John Carroll, Priest." [33] Thus, in keeping with the new American spirit of the love for freedom and democracy, *all the American priests elected their first bishop.* Doubtless this fact, which John Carroll as vicar apostolic vigorously promoted, was connected with the support of the lay trustee system by Bishop Carroll.

Bishop Carroll attempted to perpetuate the custom of having the bishop elected by the priests, but with only very limited success. In 1792 a synod of all the clergy was held and requested Rome either to set up another diocese in the United States or allow Bishop Carroll a coadjutor bishop. In writing about the request, Carroll reported: "It is proposed to the Propaganda to allow the ten oldest clergymen here, and five others to be nominated by myself, to be the electors of the new bishop, ordinary or coadjutor." [34] According to Guilday's paraphrase, Rome was unwilling to grant the form of an election of the new bishop by priests, although the substance of the request was allowed in that instance: "Moreover, the privilege (*pro hac vice tantum*) granted in his own election, could hardly be permitted a second time by the Holy, even though, as Carroll had pointed out, a direct appointment by Rome might be interpreted by the enemies of the Church in the Republic as violating the spirit of the Constitution. Antonelli urged Carroll to consult with the older priests of his diocese and to suggest the name of a worthy candidate for the coadjutorship." [35] The man chosen, and subsequently appointed by Rome, Laurence Graessl, unfortunately died before he was consecrated. The same electoral procedure was again followed, for "on October 18, 1794, Dr. Carroll wrote to Antonelli from Philadelphia, that the choice of the clergy had fallen upon a man . . . ," Leonard Neale.[36]

These bishops were the last elected, formally or informally, by American priests. Following the behest of Rome, Carroll did not use any electoral form in arriving at the next three names to be submitted to Rome for new bishoprics but rather consulted his priests informally. Then in 1808 for the first time a bishop (Richard Concanon) was appointed to an American see without American recommendation. As a result, in an attempt to head off foreign influence (Irish, French, or Roman) in the appointment of future American bishops, at the 1810 convention of the American bishops a request was sent to Rome: "In the case the Holy See will graciously permit the nomination to vacant bishoprics to be made in the United States, it is humbly and respectfully suggested to the supreme pastor of the Church to allow the nomination for vacant dioceses to proceed solely from the Archbishop and Bishops of this Ecclesiastical Province." [37] Thus the focus of the struggle over the selecting of the new American bishops was shifted away from whether they should be elected by priests or not, to whether they should be nominated by American bishops or non-American elements.

The seesaw struggle between American bishops and Rome and others continued for the next two decades. After having the American nominees rejected in favor of three Irish priests by Rome in 1820, Archbishop Maréchal of Baltimore complained to the Vatican, but was "rather contemptuously informed that neither the Archbishop of Baltimore nor his suffragans had the right to nominate the vacant sees." [38] Maréchal then appealed to the pope personally and appeared to win his case, for a decree was ordered prepared that would give the American bishops the right to *nominate* new bishops. However, a Father Inglesi, who had been suggested by Bishop Du Bourg of New Orleans as his coadjutor, was discovered

at Rome at that time to be something less than he
claimed. Consequently the decree as it was issued June 3,
1822, granted American bishops only the right to *recommend* men to bishoprics.[39] This general principle was
consolidated when in 1834 Rome approved the detailed
plan for recommendations drawn up by the Second Provincial Council of Baltimore, 1833. Basically the plan
was that each bishop should draw up a terna, or list of
three names, in order of preference and send them to the
senior bishop and to the Congregation of Propaganda,
with the reasons for their recommendations. The Congregation was careful to add at the end of the decree:
"It wishes to emphasize the fact, that the names thus
sent are not really nominations, elections or requests,
but properly and solely recommendations, imposing no
obligation on the Congregation to select any of the candidates mentioned." [40] All discussion of priests' voice in the
selection of bishops was absent.

Thus, in the second quarter of the nineteenth century,
as the status of the laity vis à vis the clergy reached a
low ebb, where it remained for decades, so also did the
status of the priests vis à vis the bishops. In 1852 Abbot
Boniface Wimmer, O.S.B., the founder of the Benedictines
in America, wrote: "The will of the bishop is the only
law. . . . Accordingly they are naturally distrustful of
every attempt to deprive them more or less of their unrestricted power, or to insure oneself against their arbitrariness." [41] Yet it was just three years later that perhaps the
first voice in decades was raised by the Eighth Provincial
Council of Baltimore in favor of giving consultors chosen
from among the priests some part in the naming of episcopal candidates—but the council made only a recommendation, not a law.[42] Still, pressure continued to
mount slowly. As the preparations for the Second Plenary
Council, 1866, proceeded, Archbishop Martin Spalding
of Baltimore, the presiding prelate at the council, indicated
his support for granting consultors from among the

priests a voice in the selection of episcopal candidates, and Archbishop Peter Richard Kenrick (who three years later was the leader of the majority American episcopal opposition to the declaration of papal infallibility) enthusiastically favored the Irish method of allowing every priest exercising the care of souls a voice in espiscopal selection.[43] Spalding even hoped to raise the consultors to the level of the European cathedral chapters of canons, but the matter got no farther than a discussion; it was not voted on. In fact, as Daniel Callahan has pointed out, the 1866 pastoral letter laid "far heavier stress on the authority of the Church and the bishops than was ever characteristic of the earlier pastorals—and this at a time when there was practically no threat whatever against the bishops' authority." [44]

In the period just before and during the first part of Vatican I, a number of articles in favor of rights for priests were printed in *Freeman's Journal* by James A. McMaster and Eugene M. O'Callaghan (the latter under the pen names "Jus" and "Ecclesiasticus"). Again, after the moderating tendencies of Pope Leo XIII began to take effect and the Third Plenary Council of Baltimore (1884) approached, more vigorous voices were heard. Father William Mahoney published in 1883 a volume detailing the reforms needed to provide priests their proper rights, and in the same year Father Patrick Corrigan published a pamphlet entitled *Episcopal Nominations,* which was immediately suppressed by his bishop. Undaunted, Corrigan published in the next year a pamphlet entitled *What the Catholic Church Most Needs in the United States, or the Voice of the Priests in the Election of Bishops.* Doubtless all this exerted pressure on the bishops to give the priests a voice in episcopal selection, but the decisive force for change came from Rome: "In the meeting at Rome, 1883, preliminary to the Third Plenary Council, the United States Prelates objected to a Cathedral Chapter as it existed in England, Ireland, and Holland.

Still, Rome insisted. A compromise was struck in the appointment of a 'universitas' of consultors with defined rights and duties. Here the voice of the clergy would be heard. The consultors and permanent rectors were representatives of the clergy in the meetings, to select men for the vacancies." [45] The council did then pass a decree granting consultors and permanent rectors the right to draw up a terna of three names in the order of preference to fill a vacancy, which list was either approved or disapproved by the bishops of the province and then forwarded to Rome. The list was only a set of recommendations, but *de facto* they were most often followed by Rome. Here was the beginning of a revival of priestly and lay responsibility in the American church at the end of the nineteenth century.

THE AMERICANIST RENAISSANCE

The flowering of the Catholic Church in the last decade and a half of the nineteenth century, often described as the "Americanist Movement," was led by a number of vigorous, open prelates, including Cardinal Gibbons of Baltimore, Archbishop Ireland of St. Paul, Bishop J. L. Spalding of Peoria, Bishop Keane, the first rector of The Catholic University of America, and Bishop O'Connell, rector of the North American College in Rome. These men and their supporters, especially the Paulist Fathers, worked for greater freedom within the church, and for a more direct, optimistic attitude in the church's relations with society in general and the state. They favored the church's coming out of the ghetto that it had shut itself in during the long pontificates of Gregory XVI (1831–1846) and Pius IX (1846–1878). This American Catholic renaissance of course corresponded in time with the Catholic renaissance that also developed in Europe at the end of the nineteenth and the beginning of the twentieth centuries: under the more benign leadership of Pope Leo XIII Catholic historical and Biblical research began to catch up with the rest of the nineteenth century; a rapprochement with the modern democratic state was begun; the involvement of the church in modern industrial and urban social problems was promoted.

The Americanist renaissance has been admirably detailed by a number of scholars, Catholic and Protestant, lay and clerical,[46] so that it is unnecessary to repeat that task here. However, it should be noted that besides the development of the open, progressive leadership on the episcopal level, and the priestly involvement in the selection of bishops mentioned above, there was also an extraordinary lay renaissance in the American Catholic Church at this time. Daniel Callahan described this phenomenon with thoroughness,[47] noting that greater responsibility for the layman was not only often written and spoken about then by both laymen and clerics, perhaps most enthusiastically by the greatest of the Americanists, Archbishop Ireland, but also acted upon in a number of ways. The peak expressions of this lay renaissance were the two national lay congresses in Baltimore and Chicago in 1889 and 1893; among other things, the two very largely successful congresses promoted greater freedom for the layman within the church, and greater involvement of the church in the social problems of the day.

But the lay renaissance and the hopes of the Americanists for a more general democratization of the church (as was specifically called for by Denis O'Connell while he was rector in Rome) and for the church's entry into the marketplace were dashed by mounting conservative opposition, which reached a first culmination, as far as America was concerned, in the letter of Leo XIII, *Testem benevolentiae,* condemning "Americanism," and an ultimate culmination in the condemnation of "modernism" by Pope Pius X. What Catholic thought in America was not suppressed by the condemnation of Americanism was absolutely crushed by the incredibly vicious ecclesiastical terrorism initiated by the antimodernist papal decrees *Pascendi* and *Lamentabili* and the Oath Against Modernism; at the end of the first, for example, it was decreed that each diocese set up a vigilance committee to meet bimonthly in secret to report on and extirpate any shred of "modernism" from among the clergy and laity. As a result, the intellectual, theological, and spiritual life of the Catholic Church in both Europe and America stagnated until after the First World War, and then only slowly recovered. The capstone on the burial of the responsibility of the priests and laity in the American church was set in place in 1916 when the right of priests to compose a terna of episcopal candidates, so painstakingly achieved in 1885, was eliminated by Rome.[48]

THE TWENTIETH CENTURY

Much could, and should, somewhere else, be written about the history of the American Catholic laity in the twentieth century: the end of the immigrations, the increase in Catholic college graduates, the founding and development of *Commonweal,* the liturgical movement, the lay apostolate, etc. But suffice it to say here that progress in freedom and responsibility for the laity was very slow in this country, being much more spoken of than acted upon. The same is also basically true for priests as far as their rights and responsibilities vis à vis the bishops are concerned; in the matter of selecting new bishops the priests continued to have no voice. In fact, even the American bishops suffered a partial eclipse in this area. An apostolic delegate (Rome's man in Washington) was appointed to the United States about the turn of the century, and subsequently wielded great influence, along with a very few conservative, powerful

American prelates (such as Cardinal Spellman), in the appointment of new bishops.[49]

But Vatican II caused a dramatic turn of affairs in America, as in the church universal. Freedom and responsibility for all the people of God was promoted mightily in word at the Council. However, when the American bishops, as was the case with many other national hierarchies, returned home from the Council, their euphoria for collegiality most often suddenly congealed. Still, the theologians and many of the clergy and laity have tended to take the Council at face value and have promoted a whole variety of developments in priestly and lay initiative: priests' associations have been set up on local and national levels, as have also lay organizations and ecumenical groups; parish councils with various degrees of responsibility and effectiveness have been established in many, though far from all, areas; some few dioceses have erected pastoral councils, representing laity and clergy, again with differing responsibility and effectiveness; recently the diocese of Detroit put into effect a constitution by which the diocese is to be governed, which entails a variety of representation and responsibility for priests and laity and even contains a careful grievance procedure (John England redivivus).

Nevertheless, these developments in America have been painfully sporadic and snail-paced. In the matter of priests, let alone laity, having a part in the selection of bishops almost no progress has been made, except in the growing awareness of the possibility and desirability of such participation.[50] In some few instances priests and laity have been invited by their bishop to express their wishes in the selection of new bishops.[51]

Conclusion

Looking back over the 180-year history of the Catholic Church in the United States it can be seen that it began with a high level of concern for the freedom and responsibility of the priests and laity, including their having a serious part in the selection of their leaders; that this concern passed through a dark night of the senses until the latter part of the nineteenth century, when the charisma of Americanism burst upon it; that it then entered a dark night of the soul for two thirds of a century, only to come face to face with the sudden glory of Vatican II. However, like the saint ascending Mount Carmel, the Catholic Church can fail to cooperate adequately with this grace, and what would happen then would be *corruptio optimae pessima:* the church would rapidly grow even more ineffective in the lives of more and more people. It seems clear from the extraordinary outpouring of the Spirit in recent years that we are living in an unusually graced time; but grace must be cooperated with to be translated into human events. Our history should teach us that if we do not translate the passing grace of the moment (today the encouragement of greater freedom and responsibility for the People of God) into concrete, human forms, including among others legal, political forms, we shall have inadequately responded to this grace. Specifically, all Catholics—lay, priestly, and episcopal—should press for greater participation of laity, priests, and bishops in the decision-making in the church, including the selection of their leaders, from pastor to pope.

NOTES

I. An Exchange of Letters with Bishop Josef Schoiswohl

1. Bishop Schoiswohl was the ordinary of the diocese of Graz-Seckau, Austria, during the 1950's and 1960's.

II. Limited Term of Office for Resident Bishops?

1. It is to be expressly emphasized that the concern of our suggestion is primarily a limitation of the term of office in general; only secondarily does the question of the precise length of the term enter in.

III. Election of Bishops as a New Desideratum in Church Practice

1. *Codex Iuris Canonici,* canon 329, par. 2; cf. canon 332, par. 1.

2. Here too a confirming inquiry with the political government must be undertaken to ascertain whether political considerations exist against the future leader of the diocese. On this, cf. J. Kaiser, *Die politische Klausel der Konkordate* (Berlin, 1949).

3. Cf. K. Mörsdorf, *Lehrbuch des Kirchenrechts auf Grund des Codex Iuris Canonici* I (Munich, 1964), pp. 409 f. On the dispute in the election of the successor to Bishop Franziskus von Streng of Basel, cf. E. Isele, "Postskriptum zur Kontroverse um das Baseler Bischofswahlrecht," in *Schweizer Rundschau* 12 (1967). The opposite position is advocated by Helveticus, "Bedrohte Freiheit der Baseler Bischofswahl?" in *Civitas* 22 (1967), pp. 537–541; by the same author see "Unbeantwortete Fragen zur Baseler Bischofswahl," in *Vaterland* 64 (March 17, 1967); also, "Nochmals: Bedrohte Freiheit der Baseler Bischofswahl? Eine Stellungnahme des Ordinariates des Bistums Basel und eine Antwort von 'Helveticus,' " in *Luzerner Neueste Nachrichten* 65 (March 18, 1967). In this context it is not necessary to go into the proceedings of the Basel controversy. What is of interest is the argumentation of E. Isele that the separation of the actual election of the episcopal candidates from its announcement, along with the informative procedure in between—which was desired by Rome—was a purely intraecclesial transaction that did not touch the church-state agreements. The purely formal side of this argumentation of course obviously is supportive of the petitions in episcopal elections as they have occurred in Germany and elsewhere recently; for, one can say objectively and *sine ira et studio,* what is correct for a centralized procedure, under the same presuppositions must be reasonable for a democratic one.

4. K. Mörsdorf, in *Lexikon für Theologie und Kirche* II (Freiburg, 1958).

5. The term "ordained Christians" should replace the idea of "priest," which has become misleading in our usage. The same thing is true for the terms "presbyter" or "congregational leader," used in the course of this report. Cf. G. Biemer, "Hat der Klerus noch eine Zukunft?" in *Diakonia* 4 (1969), pp. 23–35, esp. p. 34.

6. Cyprian, Epistle 68, 2; cf. Epistles 65, 8; 67, 5; 69, 5, etc.

7. Yves Congar, *Der Laie* (Stuttgart, 1956), p. 391. [The English translation *Lay People in the Church* (The Newman Press, 1957) is an abbreviation of the original. This quotation should appear on page 233, but doesn't.] Bibli-

ographical references for this topic are found in the German version of Congar [omitted in English], pp. 387–393. Cf. also K. Bihemeyer and H. Tüchle, *Kirchengeschichte* I (Paderborn, 1956), pp. 108 f.; J. Daniélou and H. Morrou, *The Christian Centuries* I (McGraw-Hill Book Company, Inc., 1964), pp. 475 ff.; Karl Baus, *From the Apostolic Community to Constantine* (New York, 1965), pp. 498 ff. On the canonical aspects, cf. Mörsdorf, *Lehrbuch des Kirchenrechts* . . . I, p. 409.

8. Leo I, Epistle 10, 4 (*Patrologia Latina*, Vol. 54, p. 628). Cf. also the formulation traced back to Celestine I: "No bishop should be installed against the will of the people" (Epistle 4, 5; *PL* 50.434). See also the contribution of P. Stockmeier in this volume, in which the patristic witnesses are evaluated in detail.

9. Out of the multitude of pertinent contributions, cf. J. Ratzinger, "Die pastoralen Implikationen der Lehre von der Kollegialität der Bischöfe," in *Concilium* I (1965), pp. 16–29; J. Neumann, "Die Rechtsprinzipien des II. Vatikanischen Konzils als Kritik an der traditionellen Kanonistik," in *Theologische Quartalschrift* 147 (1967), pp. 257–292; E. Golomb, "Kollegialität als Strukturprinzip der Kirche," in *Lebendige Seelsorge* 19 (1968), pp. 157–162; G. Biemer, "Einheit und Zeugnis," in *Oberrheinisches Pastoralblatt* 69 (1968), pp. 193–197.

10. Neumann, *loc. cit.*, p. 263.

11. Golomb, *loc. cit.*, p. 161.

12. Cf. G. Biemer, "Glaubenszeugnis als Ziel des Dienstes der Kirche," in *Theologische Quartalschrift* 148 (1968), pp. 303–321, esp. p. 318.

13. Cf. the detailed theological exposition in the contribution of H. Küng in this volume.

14. Cf. *Lumen gentium* 13, 35; *Apostolicam actuositatem*, 6, 10, 11.

15. *Lumen gentium* 11; *Sacrosanctum concilium* 33.

16. Cf. *Apostolicam actuositatem* 10, 25; *Gaudium et spes* 43.

17. *Apostolicam actuositatem* 10.

18. *Lumen gentium* 37.

19. *Ibid.*

20. Concerning the sources of the following presentation it

should be noted that the material to a great extent exists in correspondence that was placed at my disposal or is from newspaper articles in the daily press or from my own information. The character of the sources may in part be the result of the contemporaneity of these proceedings, but is also in part because, symptomatically, no informational report of an official sort was published. In the supplement of a circular letter of the "Working Group on the Election of Bishops" of the diocese of Cologne, dated November 29, 1968, W. Kolocik of Neuss writes: "Again and again there appeared the request or demand that we completely refrain from supplying material to the press, radio, and television in this matter. This attitude has been strictly observed in the circle until now. If reports nevertheless reached the press, that never occurred by order of the circle. Even now, however, it is discussed whether the public does not have a right to information, whether we wish to move in the church farther into an area of isolation, whether the often-cited lack of objectivity of the press is a result of our abandoning the publications media to rumor and inaccuracies."

21. From the letter of Bishop J. Bluyssen of March 21, 1968, to Pastor R. Schreck, 6701 Neuhofen.

22. Cf. the *Frankfurter Allgemeine Zeitung* of March 29, 1968, and the *Rheinpfalz* of April 2, 1968.

23. *Le Monde,* February 29, 1968.

24. Cf. note 5, above. By "congregational leaders" is meant ordained Christians who either as pastors actually lead congregations, or as vicars [or assistant pastors, as they often are called in America] are potentially congregational leaders. In a communication on the meeting of the priests' council of the diocese of Rottenburg on March 11, 1969, we read among other things: "As a whole the tendency becomes clear to understand the vicar less as 'assistant priest' but rather as an independent colleague in pastoral care."

25. Cf. *Codex Iuris Canonici,* canon 436.

26. The petition was published on March 2 in the entire Palatinate press (cf. *Westpfälzische Rundschau* of March 2, 1968), and on March 10 in *Der Pilger* and in the *Neue Bildpost.*

27. From a letter from the episcopal chancery of Speyer,

signed by R. Motzenbäcker, dated March 14, 1968, to Pastor Hans Dieter Thirolf, 6650 Homburg.

28. "In a communication to the Chapter Vicar of Speyer, the Apostolic Nuncio for Germany states that the Holy See cannot deviate from the rule that is valid for the entire Catholic Church; moreover, it must restrict itself to the prescriptions of the present German concordat" (*Der Pilger* of March 17, 1968).

29. *Rheinpfalz* on March 11, 1968; cf. *Der Pilger* of March 17, 1968.

30. Reported in a condensed form by the *Frankfurter Allgemeine Zeitung,* March 28, 1968.

31. In April of 1968 there was formed in the diocese of Cologne a "Working Group on the Election of Bishops," to which originally five and later sixty ordained Christians belonged. Its purpose was that, concerning the successor of Cardinal Frings, "all priests of the archdiocese participate by making suggestions for the drawing up of the list of names for this high office" (communication of the Working Group to the nuncio, Archbishop C. Bafile, Bad Godesberg, on June 19, 1968). This concern was made known with a petition to the nunciature signed by 72 priests of the diocese. On October 18, 1968, the Working Group organized a written inquiry among all the congregational leaders of the diocese of Cologne. On the question of whether they wished to participate in the appointment of the bishop, of the 441 persons queried, 86 percent replied in the affirmative, 12 percent in the negative, and 2 percent gave no answer. In a reportorial account of the Working Group on November 29, 1968, from which the preceding data were gathered, the noteworthy engagement of the congregational leaders was explained by, among other things, the following pressing concerns: "The resignation of many of our brethren, the paralysis of much individual initiative by the structures, the one-sided obligation of obedience, the distrust of one another and especially of 'those above,' errors in leadership that have to be paid for by those below without showing a reaction or yielding results (e.g., the question of schools), a lack of cooperation between the parish, deanery, and diocesan levels (territorial and categorical)."

The problem of the election of the bishop in Cologne was supposedly settled by another route—through the appointment of a coadjutor. In a letter to me dated February 24, 1969, the provost of the Cologne cathedral, Dr. C. Gielen, says among other things "that the local chapter has no statutes for episcopal election. The election is conducted according to the stipulations of the agreement of the state of Prussia with the Holy See on June 14, 1929, Art. 6. Although this mode is not designed for the election of a coadjutor, the Holy See nevertheless also observed these stipulations in the appointment a few months ago." Certainly it is not out of place to ask why the law governing church-state relations, which was certainly not pertinent in this case, was observed, but not the very pertinent and vital desire of the collaborators of the future bishop.

In this way, not only the efforts of the "Working Group on Episcopal Elections" of Cologne, but, in another manner, the preparations of the *Conseil presbytéral* of Fribourg, Switzerland, elected upon the episcopal mandate of Bishop Charrièr on November 21, 1968, were frustrated. In the two meetings of the council on March 11 and May 27, 1968, the speaker, supported by a great number of members, demanded that in the event of an episcopal appointment (*nomination d'un évêque*) previous consultations take place. With this understanding the chairman of the council had prepared a plan on July 4, 1968, for the possible questioning of ordained and nonordained Christians in the diocese in the event of episcopal vacancy. (On this, cf. "Protocoles officiels des réunions du Conseil presbytéral des 11 mars et 27 mai 1968.") In the midst of this preparatory work there burst on July 22, 1968, the news that a new coadjutor of the diocese, Monsignor Mamie, had been named. The agitation over this proceeding in the *Conseil presbytéral* as well as among other members of the diocese is certainly not incomprehensible. (On further developments, cf.: "Rapport de la présidence du Conseil presbytéral à l'Assemblée du 30 septembre 1968"; and "Protocole officiel de l'Assemblée du 30 septembre 1968.")

32. Münster is discussed later in this essay.

33. Cf. *Herder-Korrespondenz* 23 (1969), p. 57; *Christ in der Gegenwart* 21 (1969), p. 58.

34. "Votum für den Priester- und Seelsorgerat der Diözese Freiburg/Brsg.," presented by the assistant pastors of the Freiburg diocese, p. 3; reported in *Diakonia* 3 (1968), pp. 284–291, esp. p. 287. Also cf. the *Frankfurter Allgemeine Zeitung* of March 28, 1968.

35. The resolutions, which were treated and passed in five working circles and then in plenary session, were labeled: questions of priestly spirituality, the inner structure of the church, personnel questions, religious instruction, continuing theological education.

36. *Bühler Vikarstreffen* I (June, 1968), p. 7; reprinted in part in *Der Seelsorger* 38 (1968), pp. 345–348, as well as in *Katechetische Blätter* 93 (1968), pp. 621–627. (The resolution on the election of bishops cited here is consequently from time to time repeated completely.) Cf. the memorandum on the route of ordination of the diocese of Rottenburg of June, 1968, in "Künftige Strukturen kirchlichen Lebens. Ziele und Wege innerdiözesaner Entwicklung," p. 4; reprinted in *Diakonia* 3 (1968), pp. 291–295, esp. p. 295. Cf. also F. J. Trost, "Demokratische Bischofswahl," in *Publik* of November 1, 1968, p. 25. While in the resolution of the assistant pastors of the state of Baden there were developed from theological considerations concrete suggestions that proceeded beyond the contemporary canonical stipulations, in a statement by the laity of the diocese of Freiburg [coterminous with the state of Baden] in June, 1968, propositions were worked out that can be realized within the framework of the existing order. The statement took positions on four subject areas: on the task and the manner of representation of laity in the church, on the reform of financial administration, on the ecclesiastical press, and on the question of episcopal elections. "Today's form of episcopal elections, as it is laid down in the general and local legal prescriptions, is an expression of an outdated conception. We ask to be involved in a new understanding in which the New Testament teaching of the People of God and its communal concern for ecclesiastical service, as it was expressed in the assertions of the church fathers and in almost a thousand years of practice, will again be realized in timely form. For the transitional period until this reform is accomplished we demand a participation (compatible with the still valid legal

prescriptions) of the priests and laity in the procedure of episcopal election in such a way that the cathedral chapter in the diocese of Freiburg, which vis à vis the Holy See has the right of selection, share the election in the inner-church area with priests and laity. The following rules would be possible:

"1. Suggestions for the choice to be made by the cathedral chapter are gone through by an electoral commission, which consists of the bishop, the episcopal vicars, the vicar general, and the representatives of the chapter, the priests' council, the pastoral council, and the diocesan council.

"2. The electoral commission is obligated to weigh and consider also the suggestions that are proposed and confirmed either in writing or orally by at least ten priests or lay persons of the diocese.

"3. If the cathedral chapter members, authorized as electors by the Holy See, wish to nominate candidates who are not represented on the electoral commission's list, then they ask the electoral commission to consult the list again and to express its opinion on the cathedral chapter's candidates.

"Such a collaboration of priests and laity opposes neither current church law nor the stipulations of the concordat."

37. *Bühler Vikarstreffen* II (November, 1968), p. 13. Moreover, the assistant pastors in this report of their resolutions demanded a time limitation on the individual serving functions of pastor, dean, episcopal vicar, and bishop; cf. *ibid.*, p. 14.

38. "An influence of the People of God on the designation of an office-bearer, as for example a pastor or bishop, is thus in principle not against the constitution of the church, because such a collaboration does not exclude the notion that the fullness of official power of the one so 'elected' comes from Christ and his always hierarchically understood church, and not really from the random throng of electors as such. . . . With the size of our present-day diocese and indeed of individual parishes it is hardly practical to think of a universal election, particularly since the majority of the church members cannot really be in the position to judge whether the presuppositions and characteristics necessary for the bearing of office are present in a certain candidate." Karl Rahner, *Demokratie in der Kirche?*, a lecture delivered at the Uni-

versity of Freiburg-im-Breisgau on May 3, 1968, and published in the series of the Katholischen Studentengemeinde St. Fidelis in Freiburg: *Glauben—Wissen—Bildung,* Section II, Lectures No. 37, pp. 14 f.

39. Norbert Greinacher, "Wege der Wandlung zu einer brüderlichen kollegialen Kirche," in *Lebendige Seelsorge* 19 (1968), pp. 168–176, esp. pp. 174 f.; also his "Für eine neue Gemeindeordnung," in *Der Seelsorger* 38 (1968), pp. 291–295, esp. p. 294.

40. H. Küng, *Truthfulness: The Future of the Church* (Sheed & Ward, Inc., 1968), pp. 172 f. See also his essay in this volume.

41. *Rheinpfalz* of March 4, 1968; cf. *Neue Bildpost* of March 10, 1968.

42. *Rheinpfalz* of May 4, 1968.

43. Letter of Pastor H. Huesmann of St. Mauritz Church in Münster to the priests' council, December 27, 1968.

44. P. Wesemann, "Münster vor der Bischofswahl," in *Forum* 1 (1969), pp. 1–2.

45. M. Breitschaft, "Der vakante Bischofsstuhl—Chance der Erneuerung? Überlegungen zur Ernennung und Person eines neuen Bischofs," in *Termine—Berichte—Meinungen* (published by the working circle "Information" in the Catholic Student Congregation of Münster), 1 (1969), pp. 1–3, esp. p. 2.

46. See also H. Herles, "Wie man neuerdings Bischof wird. Zum Beispiel in Münster," in *Frankfurter Allgemeine Zeitung* of February 22, 1969, p. 2.

47. See also what Yves Congar says on the testimony of the role of the laity: "The subject is very important and very delicate, and cannot be touched otherwise than in the only light proper to it: that of the Church's tradition, which in a manner of this kind is expressed by actual facts at least as much as in doctrinal texts." *Lay People in the Church,* p. 231.

48. Cf. Congar, *Der Laie,* p. 391; see above, note 7.

49. See the contributions of H. Küng and P. Stockmeier in this volume. Also P. Stockmeier, "Von der Diakonie zur Hierarchie. Zum Wandel des Amtsverständnisses im Frühchristentum," in *Orientierung* 32 (1968), pp. 259–261.

50. Acts 6:3–7. Cf. on the other hand Congar, *Der Laie,* p. 389; see above, note 7.

51. The diverging opinions in the concrete suggestions on this point are obvious. In principle, Karl Rahner's denial of a universal election will find general assent (*op. cit.*, p. 15). The statement of the assistant pastors and the laity in Baden considered a group of at least ten members of the diocese as authorized to make recommendations (see note 36). P. Wesemann, on the contrary, says: "I do not share the opinion of the meeting of assistant pastors at Bühl that such suggestions may only 'be worked out and presented by societies and discussion groups'; the well-thought-out suggestion coming from an individual seems at least as valuable to me," *loc. cit.*, p. 2.

IV. ELECTION AND LIMITATION OF TERM OF OFFICE IN CANON LAW

1. Cf. the article by Peter Stockmeier in this volume; also F. A. Staudenmaier, *Geschichte der Bischofswahlen mit besonderer Berücksichtigung der Rechte und des Einflusses christlicher Fürsten* (Tübingen, 1830); P. Hinschius, *System des katholischen Kirchenrechts* II (Graz, 1959), pp. 512–688; F. X. Funk, "Die Bischofswahl im christlichen Altertum und im Anfang des Mittelalters," in *Kirchengeschichtliche Abhandlungen und Untersuchungen* I (Paderborn, 1897), pp. 23–39.

2. Cf. Hinschius, *System* . . . II, p. 522; J. B. Sägmüller, "Die Papstwahl durch das Kardinalskolleg als Prototyp der Bischofswahl durch das Domkapitel," in *Theologische Quartalschrift* 97 (1915), pp. 321–336, esp. pp. 322 f.

3. Cf. Hinschius, *System* . . . I, p. 227; J. B. Sägmüller, "Die Ernennung des Nachfolgers durch die Päpste Ende des fünften und Anfang des sechsten Jahrhunderts," in *Theologische Quartalschrift* 85 (1903), pp. 91–108, 235–254, esp. pp. 243–245.

4. The undisputed Synod of Antioch (341) provided in canon 23: "A bishop is not allowed to appoint his own successor, even when he is approaching the end of his life. If he does so it is invalid. Rather the canonical rule is to be strictly adhered to which prescribes that a bishop may not be appointed except by the synod and after the judgment of the bishops. . . ." (Cf. C. J. von Hefele, *Conciliengeschichte* [Freiburg, 1873], I, pp. 601–602.) The Council of Nicaea (325) already had ordained in canon 8 that there could not

be two bishops in one city. Cf. H. Jedin, *Conciliorum Oecumenicorum Decreta* (1962), p. 9.

5. Council of Nicaea (325), canon 15. Even at this synod the participants included several esteemed bishops who had left their bishoprics and taken on others (cf. Hefele, *op. cit.*, p. 483).

6. Cf. Decretals of Gregory IX, Book I, title 6, canon 2: The decisive words *"nisi de hoc poenituerit"* were first interpolated into the wording of canon 2 of the Council of Sardica (342) by Raymond of Peñafort (d. 1275). (Cf. Hefele, *op. cit.*, p. 648; Ae. Friedberg, *Corpus Iuris Canonici* II [1959], 49 Tit. VI, Cap. II, note 10.)

7. Cf. Decretals of Gregory IX, Book I, title 7, canon 2; also, J. Trummer, "Mystisches im alten Kirchenrecht. Die geistige Ehe zwischen Bischof und Diözese," in *Österreichisches Archiv für Kirchenrecht* 2 (1951), pp. 62–75.

8. Cf. Trummer, *loc. cit.*, p. 65; J. A. Eidenschink, *The Election of Bishops in the Letters of Gregory the Great* (The Catholic University of America Press, 1945), pp. 95–96, 146.

9. Also known as Martin II. He was the son of the presbyter Palumbus of Gallese (Tuscany) and bishop of Caere in Etruria. Cf. M. Heimbucher, *Papstwahlen unter den Karolingern* (1889), pp. 187 ff. Even if Gregory of Nazianzus already in the year 382 numbered the prohibition of transfers among the long-dead laws, this prohibition was strictly observed in the Latin Church even into the ninth century. In this way the more fitted were often excluded from the office of bishop of Rome.

[10. In the United States, of course, many bishops were ordinaries in dioceses before their present ones—including, for example, Cardinals Dearden, Cody, Carberry, and Wright (who is now in Rome).]

11. *Christus Dominus* 3.3.

12. Cf. Ph. Hofmeister, "Die kanonischen und nichtkanonischen Wahlen," in *Zeitschrift für Katholische Theologie* 77 (1955), pp. 432–471; M. Kaiser, *sub* "Wahl," in *Lexikon für Theologie und Kirche* (2d ed.); Ph. Hofmeister, *sub* "Wahlrecht," in *ibid.*

13. Nevertheless the constitution on papal elections of 1904 was actually replaced by a new one by Pius XII in

1945. This too has been altered in a few points by a *motu proprio* issued by John XXIII on May 9, 1962.

14. In reference to the appointment of the synodal examiners and the parish consultors, we find it is not really concerned with an election in the actual sense, but rather with the form of an assent or rejection of the bishop's suggestion (canon 385, par. 1). The synod thus has no electoral right, but only a right of veto (cf. Mörsdorf, *Lehrbuch des Kirchenrechts auf Grund des Codex Iuris Canonici* I (Munich, 1964), p. 437. The same holds true for the appointment of the synodal judges (canon 1574).

15. Hofmeister, "Die kanonischen und nichtkanonischen Wahlen," *loc. cit.*, p. 439.

16. Cf. W. Ülhof, "Die Pfarrwahl in der Erzdiözese Paderborn," in *Westfälische Zeitschrift* 109 (1959), pp. 295–341, 355.

17. In the rest of Europe, elections for this ecclesiastical office were not able to develop properly because of their special genesis. From the end of the Middle Ages and the decline of collegial thinking, the right of the lord of the manor in appointments or suggestions predominated: cf. F. X. Künstle, *Die deutsche Pfarrei und ihr Recht zu Ausgang des Mittelalters* (1963), esp. pp. 42–69. Here there were especially important rights of cooperation of the congregation: cf. D. Kurze, *Pfarrerwahlen im Mittelalter* (1966), which specially points up the variety of the possibilities in constitutional law (3:314 f.; 352). Here it is to be observed that election to ecclesiastical offices in the cities—like other auxiliary rights—did not belong to the faithful as a whole and as faithful, but rather to the autonomous body of the (secular) congregation: "Within the city walls the ecclesiastical person should be subordinate to the civil regulations set up by the council and citizenry." Cf. A. Werminghoff, *Verfassungsgeschichte der Deutschen Kirche im Mittelalter* (1913), p. 98.

18. Nevertheless, in many Eastern churches the original forms are still retained unchanged; cf., e.g., K. Zapotoczky, "Pfarrerwahlen in Syrien," in *Der Seelsorger* 36 (1966), pp. 426–428. The Roman law for the "uniate" Eastern churches does not make any provision for the right of election of the pastor (canon 496, *Jus Orientalium Personarum* of 1957).

19. The very dissimilar conditions of the most diverse religious orders and societies made it necessary that the *Codex Iuris Canonici* establish only the bare outlines of law for them: cf. Ph. Hofmeister, "Die Orden soberen im Kodex," *Archiv für katholisches Kirchenrecht* 1926 (1954), p. 332; P. Tocanel, "De facultate superioris confirmandi vel repellendi electum," in *Appollinaris* 35 (1962), pp. 266–284.

20. Cf. N. Hilling, "Zur Abtswahl der Benediktinerregel," in *Archiv für Katholisches Kirchenrecht* 102 (1922), pp. 55–57.

21. Cf. V. Dammertz, *Das Verfassungsrecht der Benediktinischen Mönchskongregationen* (1963), p. 157. Also H. S. Mayer, *Benediktinisches Ordensrecht in der Beuroner Kongregation* IV/2 (1936), pp. 77 f., in which it is seen that the two assistant abbots are elected by the general chapter.

22. G. Hoffmann, "Wahlen und Ämterbesetzung in der Kirche," in *Festschrift für E. Ruppel*, ed. by H. Brunotte, K. Müller, and R. Smend (1968), pp. 164–165.

23. Cf. F. Heiner, *Katholisches Kirchenrecht* II (1913), p. 184: "For the *beneficia maiora* the canonical election is the general legal form; an exception by way of particular law is found in the so-called *nominatio regio*. . . ." Nevertheless the free right of appointment by the pope had in fact become the dominant practice and had in this way attained the character of "law by custom." Already in the year 1909, U. Stutz asserted: "Unlike the situation in the ancient church and in the High Middle Ages, today . . . the free conferring of the bishoprics by the pope is the rule"; *Der neuste Stand des deutschen Bischofswahlrechts* (1909), p. 116, and similarly pp. 33 f.

24. Cf. Hinschius, *System* . . . II, pp. 657 ff.; Ae. L. Richter, *Lehrbuch des katholischen und evangelischen Kirchenrechts* (1853), pp. 264–267; G. Phillips, *Lehrbuch des Kirchenrechts* I (1859), pp. 367–385, esp. p. 373; Heiner, *op. cit.*, pp. 190–201 f.

25. Stutz, *op. cit.*, p. 4.

26. K. Mörsdorf, *Das neue Besetzungsrecht der bischöflichen Stühle unter besonderer Berücksichtigung des Listenverfahrens* (1933), p. 122.

27. *Christus Dominus*, 20.2.

28. K. Mörsdorf is correct in pointing out that the refer-

ence to the right of suffrage, particularly in the first passage, has a peculiar concern, because the election of bishops, insofar as it still persists, does not lie in the hands of the state, but of an ecclesiastical organ (in *Lexikon für Theologie und Kirche* II *sub* "Vat. Konz. II," p. 186, n. 12).

29. The personal rights granted to the Eastern uniate churches by Rome in the *motu proprio* of December 6, 1957, *Cleri sanctitati,* cannot be gone into here because of lack of space. However, we must point out that this right only theoretically postulates the free right of appointment on the part of the pope. For the bishops subordinate to a patriarch it is without exception that they are elected by the electoral synod: *"Episcopi canonice eliguntur in Synodo ad normam canonum . . ."* (canon 251, *Jus Orientalium Personarum*). After the election the *confirmatio* is to be obtained from the bishop of Rome. If, however, the election takes place on the basis of a list put forward by the electoral synod and sanctioned by the Holy See, the ordination and enthronement can follow immediately. In such a case the Holy See must merely be apprised of the result of the election (canon 254, *Jus Orientalium Personarum*).

30. In Bavaria the cathedral chapter of the vacant diocese does have the right to submit to the Holy See a list of suitable candidates. And although the other Bavarian bishops as well as the other Bavarian chapters also have the right to convey lists, the pope nevertheless has "full freedom" to select from these lists a personality pleasing to him (Bavarian Concordat, Art. 14, par. 1).

31. On the basis of Art. 14, par. 1, of the Reichskonkordat, certain regulations hold for the occupancy of the episcopal seats of Rottenburg and Mainz as well as for the bishopric of Meissen and of Freiburg. Thus, apart from Bavaria, a remnant of suffrage remains to the German cathedral chapter through the legal concordat.

32. Cf. J. Funk, *Einführung in das Missionsrecht* (1958), pp. 46–52; G. Vromant, *Jus missionarium. De personis* (1935), pp. 61–193.

33. *Christus Dominus* 21.

34. The right was conceded to the monasteries of this congregation in 1880 to elect their abbot for life (cf. Dam-

mertz, *op. cit.,* p. 98). However, the Celestines, who had accepted the Benedictine Rule under Peter Morus, who later became Pope Celestine V in 1294, already recognized a term of office of only three years for abbot; cf. B. Hegglin, *Der benediktinische Abt in rechtsgeschichtlicher Entwicklung und geltendem Kirchenrecht* (1961), p. 71. Likewise in the congregation of Solesmes—in the nineteenth century—the abbots had to present themselves to their monasteries for a vote of confidence every three years (Dammertz, *op. cit.,* p. 93).

35. Cf. Mayer, *op. cit.* II/1 (1932), p. 111; Dammertz, *op. cit.,* p. 224; Hegglin, *op. cit.,* pp. 74–77. Among the Olivetans it was only at the end of the nineteenth century that the lifelong term of office for the abbot was reintroduced (cf. Dammertz, *op. cit.,* p. 101). The presidents of the congregations were elected likewise only for three, six, or twelve years (Dammertz, *op. cit.,* p. 188).

36. Abbot Cuthbert Butler was abbot of the Downside Abbey in England in the first portion of the twentieth century: *Benedictine Monachism* (London, 1924).

37. According to a decision of the Congregation of the Religious on February 25, 1922, even the founder of a society does not have the right to occupy the office of superior general for life, or to be reelected unless the constitutions so provide or he has received a special apostolic indult. In reference to women superior generals, including abbesses, the same Congregation determined on March 9, 1920, that more than one reelection must not be permitted in the rule. Cf. S. Mayer, *Neueste Kirchenrechtssammlung* I (1953), pp. 179–181.

38. Hofmeister, "Die Ordensoberen in Kodex," *loc. cit.,* pp. 337–340.

39. The limitation on the term of office decreed for the prelates and officials of the Roman Curia by the curial reform of Paul VI cannot be treated here due to the lack of space. On this subject cf. H. Schmitz, *Kurienreform* (1968), esp. pp. 27 and 161. Yet it is worth noting that the local bishops recently appointed to the Curia (in accord with the *motu proprio* of August 6, 1967, *Pro comperto sane,* No. VI), as well as the higher curial officials (i.e., the cardinals in their character as members of the congregations and the

secretaries of the congregations in accord with the apostolic constitution of August 15, 1967, *Regimini Ecclesiae* 2.5), are called only for a term of five years. Moreover, a definitive end of their term is established for the latter: according to the *Regolamento generale della Curia Romana* of February 22, 1968, Art. 23, par. 1, the superior prelates as a rule withdraw from curial service at the beginning of their seventy-fifth year; the higher and lower officials retire after the completion of their seventieth year (Art. 24, par. 1). For the auditors of the Sacred Roman Rota the old law that provides for their retirement at the age of seventy-five (Apostolic Constitution of Pius XI, *Ad incrementum,* of August 15, 1934) remains valid. In sum, in those ecclesiastical offices in which the ability to function stands in the foreground and which do not have to suffer under a sacral mystification, current law already provides for a limitation of the term of office!

40. Statistics which my colleague Prof. H. Strecker has kindly drawn up and for which I am now indebted show that in Germany since 1930 the average age of appointment has been about 54 years, the average term of office 19 years, and the average stay in one diocese about 16 years.

That means that with a limitation of the term of office of local bishops to eight years, the number of bishops would double in 16 years (the current stay in one diocese) and thus would correspond to the present overall number of reigning bishops, auxiliary bishops, resigned bishops, and those serving in the Curia. By taking 19 years as a basic term of office, of course, the number of nonruling bishops as over against the present state would grow by perhaps one third. This increase would be justifiable, however, first in the face of the growing number of tasks and secondly on the assumption that in such a development the auxiliary bishops for the most part could be taken from among the former local bishops. (With broader figures to work with, if occasion arises, the problem growing out of a limited term of office for bishops will have to be investigated separately. For the assembling of the statistical materials I am indebted to the university assistants Chr. Keller, J. Kutschka, and E. Seifert.)

V. Congregation and Episcopal Office in the Ancient Church

1. Canon 1558 of the *Codex Iuris Canonici*, in referring to the types of cases (listed in canon 1557) restricted to the Holy See states: "In causes concerning those in 1556, 1557, the incompetence of other judges is *absolute*." On the history and theology of the episcopate, see F. Prat and E. Valton, "Evêques," in *Dictionnaire de théologie catholique* V, pp. 1656–1725; H. W. Beyer and H. Karpp, "Bischof," in *Reallexikon für Antike und Christentum* II, pp. 394–407.

2. C. J. von Hefele, "Die Bischofs-Wahlen in den ersten christlichen Jahrhunderten," in *Beiträge zur Kirchengeschichte, Archäologie und Liturgik* I (Tübingen, 1864), pp. 140–144; F. X. Funk, "Die Bischofswahl im christlichen Altertum und im Anfang des Mittelalters," in *Kirchengeschichtliche Abhandlungen und Untersuchungen* I (Paderborn, 1897), pp. 23–29.

3. Yves Congar, *Lay People in the Church* (The Newman Press, 1957), p. 234.

4. H. Zimmermann, *Papstabsetzungen des Mittelalters* (Graz-Vienna-Cologne), 1968.

5. *Ibid.*, p. 6.

6. H. Zimmermann himself notes that the collaboration in the election also includes the claim to decide on the continuance in office in the case of failure (p. 10). But precisely therein lies an essential criterion that had been already developed and exercised by the ancient church.

7. See H. W. Beyer, *sub* "diakoneō ktl.," in *Theologisches Wörterbuch zum Neuen Testament* II, pp. 81–93.

8. On this passage, see E. Haenchen, *Die Apostelgeschichte* (Göttingen, 1961), pp. 122 ff. and 213 ff.

9. On the transaction and on ordination in general, see E. Lohse, *Die Ordination im Spätjudentum und im Neuen Testament* (Göttingen, 1951), pp. 74 ff.

10. Cf. F. Grau, *Der neutestamentliche Begriff Charisma. Seine Geschichte und seine Theologie* (Dissertation, Tübingen, 1946); J. Brosch, *Charismen und Ämter in der Urkirche* (Bonn, 1951). For a comparison between charis-

matic authority and occupancy of the *prima sedes,* see A. M. Koeniger, "Prima sedes a nemine iudicatur," in *Beiträge zur Geschichte des christlichen Altertums und der byzantinischen Literatur* (Festgabe A. Ehrhard; Freiburg, 1922), pp. 273–300.

11. Didache 12.1. For a view of antiquity (and also of superstition), where right means the great and noble, and left the low and weak, cf. O. Nussbaum, "Die Bedeutung von Rechts und Links in der römischen Liturgie," in *Jahrbuch für Antike und Christentum* 5 (1962), pp. 158–171.

12. Verse 44.6 repeats the reproach: "For we see that you few have driven them from their office which they had administered blamelessly in honor, although they led a good life."

13. F. Kober, *Die Deposition und Degradation nach den Grundsätzen des kirchlichen Rechts* (Tübingen, 1867), pp. 1 f. Also, H. von Campenhausen comes to the conclusion: "The bishops thus were not flatly declared 'undeposable'; only a baseless deposition, a deposition without demonstrated guilt, counted as gross injustice—something that contradicted the essence of the office and its solemn institution in the congregation." *Kirchliches Amt und geistliche Vollmacht in den ersten drei Jahrhunderten* (Tübingen, 1963), p. 101.

14. Cf. Didache 15.1; Hippolytus, Apostolic Tradition 2.

15. Such as 21.6, and other places.

16. Cf. A. d'Alès, *La théologie de Saint Cyprien* (Paris, 1922), pp. 214 ff.

17. Von Campenhausen, *op. cit.,* p. 295. The orientation of the bishop to the congregation is also characteristic of the monarchical understanding of Ignatius of Antioch; cf. Eph. 4, 1.2; Phld. 7,1; and others.

18. On this, cf. K. H. Lütcke, *"Auctoritas" bei Augustin. Mit einer Einleitung zur römischen Vorgeschichte des Begriffs* (Stuttgart, 1968), pp. 57 f.

19. Epistle 67, 3: "The people itself has the power of choosing worthy priests or of refusing unworthy ones" (*"plebs . . . ipsa habeat potestatem uel eligendi dignos sacerdotes uel indignos recusandi"*); *Corpus scriptorum ecclesiasticorum latinorum* (cited hereafter as *CSEL*) 3.2.737 ff. The concept *"potestas"* appears to refer to a legal claim

that is proper to the people in the matter of an episcopal election; cf. Lütke, *op. cit.*, pp. 29 ff. In fact, even more often Cyprian stresses the role of the people in the appointment of bishops; cf. esp. Epistle 67, 4–5 (*CSEL* 3.2.738 ff.); Epistle 58, 5–6 (*CSEL* 3.2.672 ff.). Origen shows a critical reserve toward these electoral proceedings, not least from his knowledge of some improprieties; in his homily *In numeros* XXII.4 (*Patrologia Graeca* 12.744) he demands: *"Sed discant ecclesiarum principes successores sibi non eos, qui consanguinitate generis iuncti sunt, nec qui carnis propinquitate sociantur, testamento signare neque hereditarium tradere ecclesiae principatum, sed referre ad iudicium Dei et non eligere illum, quem humanus commendat affectus, sed Dei iudicio totum de successoris electione permittere."*

20. Von Campenhausen, *op. cit.*, p. 301. He appeals to Cyprian, Epistles 19, 2; 55, 8; 67, 5.

21. Epistle 55, 8 (*CSEL* 3.2.629 ff.). [The numbering in Migne is Epistle X, 8 (*PL* III, cols. 796–797). This translation is from *The Anti-Nicene Fathers* V (Buffalo, 1886), p. 329.]

22. Th. Mommsen, *Römisches Staatsrecht* III, 1 (Leipzig, 1887), p. 402.

23. Von Hefele, "Die Bischofs-Wahlen . . . ," *loc. cit.*, p. 141.

24. F. X. Funk, "Die Bischofswahl . . . ," *loc. cit.*, p. 28.

25. See A. Beck, *Römisches Recht bei Tertullian und Cyprian, Eine Studie zur frühen Kirchenrechtsgeschichte* (Halle, 1930), pp. 130 ff.

26. Epistle 67, 5 (*CSEL* 3.2.739).

27. *Ibid.: "ordinationem iure perfectam."* The term "ordination" obviously does not mean laying on of hands, but the entire proceeding of installation; see Beck, *op. cit.*, p. 131, n. 5.

28. *Ibid.: "episcopatum, de quo fuerat iure depositus."*

29. Epistle 67, 3: *"propter quod plebs obsequens praeceptis dominicis et Deum metuens a peccatore praeposito separare se debet, nec se ad sacrilegi sacrificia miscere, quando ipsa maxime habeat potestatem uel eligendi dignos sacerdotes uel indignos rescusandi"* (*CSEL* 3.2.737); cf. note 19 above.

30. Epistle 67, 6. Also, Epistle 72, 2 (*CSEL* 3.2.776), ex-

presses the principle that priests and deacons of the Catholic Church who have joined a heretical community can be re-accepted into the parent church only as laity.

31. To this extent the suggestion of d'Alès, *"L'ordination est donc irréformable,"* can be misunderstood (*op. cit.,* p. 308). Cf. also Von Campenhausen, *op. cit.,* p. 299.

32. Hippolytus, *Philosophumena,* Book IX, Ch. VII (*The Anti-Nicene Fathers* V, p. 131).

33. Here a statement by Tertullian is noteworthy: "Enmity toward the episcopate is the mother of schisms." *De baptismo* 17.2; *Corpus Christianorum Series Latina* (Turin, 1954), I, p. 291.

34. On the problematic, see Ronald Knox, *Enthusiasm; a Chapter in the History of Religion* (Oxford University Press, Inc., 1950); also H. von Campenhausen, "Die Anfänge des Priesterbegriffs in der alten Kirche," in *Tradition und Leben. Kräfte der Kirchengeschichte* (Tübingen, 1960), pp. 272–289, esp. pp. 280 ff.

35. On the difficult state of the sources, cf. G. Touassard, "Paulos v. Samosata," in *Lexikon für Theologie und Kirche* VIII (2d ed.).

36. Eusebius, *Ecclesiastical History* VII.30.9. For an opinion, see H. U. Instinsky, *Bischofsstuhl und Kaiserthron* (Munich, 1955); a criticism of this can be found in E. Stommel, "Bischofsstuhl und höher Thron," in *Jahrbuch für Antike und Christentum* I (1958), pp. 52–78.

37. Eusebius, *Ecclesiastical History* VII. 30.19.

38. Stommel, *loc. cit.,* p. 57.

39. *Sub* "Audientia episcopalis," in *Reallexikon für Antike und Christentum.*

40. Optatus I.18: *"tunc suffragio totius populi Caecilianus eligitur et manum inponente Felice Autumnitano episcopus ordinatur,"* (*CSEL* 34.2.407); on the incident, see E. L. Grasmück, *Coercitio. Staat und Kirche im Donatistenstreit* (Bonn, 1964).

41. Optatus I.22 (*CSEL* 26.25 ff.); Augustine, Epistle 88, 1 (*CSEL* 34.2.407).

42. Augustine, Epistle 88, 5 (*CSEL* 34.2.411); Epistle 93, 13 (*CSEL* 34.2.457); Epistle 105, 8 (*CSEL* 34.2.600).

43. Presumably on the initiatives of Miltiades, fifteen more Italian bishops were called in for consultation in order to

ensure the intraecclesial recognition of the arbitration (Optatus I.23; *CSEL* 26.26 f.).

44. Eusebius, *Ecclesiastical History* X.5.21–24; Optatus, App. III (*CSEL* 26.204–206).

45. Optatus, App. V (*CSEL* 26.208–210).

46. See L. Wenger and K. Hofmann, *sub* "Absetzung" in *Reallexikon für Antike und Christentum.*

47. Also cf. canon 5 of the Council of Nicaea (325) with canon 2 of the Ecumenical Council of Constantinople (381); see C. J. von Hefele, *Conciliengeschichte* (Freiburg, 1873), I, pp. 386 ff., and II, pp. 15 ff.

48. Canon 12 of the Synod of Antioch (341) forbids any immediate recourse to the emperor; Von Hefele, *Conciliengeschichte* I, p. 517.

49. *Ibid.,* p. 237.

50. Chr. Baur, *Der heilige Johannes Chrysostomus und seine Zeit* I (Munich, 1929), pp. 147 ff.

51. Homily on Eph. 11:6 (*PG* 62.88). In the preceding section he reproaches sectarian groups: "Do you believe, I ask you, that it is enough that they call themselves orthodox if the legitimate election of the presiding officer is circumvented and made impossible?" (Homily on Eph. 11:5; *PG* 62. 86).

52. Baur, *op. cit.* II, pp. 127 ff.

53. *De sacerd.* III.11 (*PG* 48.647 f.).

54. *De sacerd.* III.11 (*PG* 48.648).

55. How strongly this principle was still established in the church of late antiquity is perhaps corroborated by the observation of Possidius on Augustine: "Truly in the priests and clerics to be ordained it was decided by the greater consensus of the Christians and following the custom of the church" (*Vita S. Augustini* 21; *PL* 32.51). Cf. also Celestine I, Epistle 4, 5: "No one is given the episcopate against his will" (*PL* 50.434); Leo I, Epistle 10, 6: "Let him who will stand before all be elected by all" (*PL* 54.634); and his Epistle 14, 5: ". . . only so that no one unwilling or unasked be ordained; so that no city will disdain or hate a bishop who was not chosen; for who is not free to have whom he wishes will be less religious than is proper" (*PL* 54.673). In this connection Congar rightly notes of M. F.-L. Ganshof, "Note sur l'élection des évêques dans l'Empire ro-

main au IV. siècle et pendant la première moitié du V.," in *Rev. internat. des droits de l'Antiquité* 5 (1950), pp. 467–498, that in the East the influence of the secular appeal in episcopal elections quickly was accepted. (*Der Laie,* p. 390, n. 50.)

56. Cf. L. Wenger, *sub* "Absetzung B. Römisch," in *Reallexikon für Antike und Christentum.*

57. On the present problematic see R. J. Bunnik, *Das Amt in der Kirche. Krise und Erneuerung in theologischer Sicht* (Düsseldorf, 1969).

VI. PARTICIPATION OF THE LAITY IN CHURCH LEADERSHIP AND IN CHURCH ELECTIONS

1. Yves Congar, *Jalons pour une théologie du laïcat* (Paris, 1953); *Lay People in the Church* (The Newman Press, 1957).

2. Cf. the very helpful article by F. Klostermann, "Allgemeine Pastoraltheologie der Gemeinde," in *Handbuch der Pastoraltheologie* III (Freiburg-Basel-Vienna, 1968), p. 43: "For this reason there also exists that fundamental collegiality and conciliarity in the congregation, the community of Christ, of which we have already spoken. Therefore no one in the church is only a presiding officer and no one is only a subordinate. Therefore behind and before every special calling in the community there is a common, basic Christian calling and a common, basic Christian status, in which everyone is reverend, excellent, and eminent, in which everyone is spiritual (Rom., ch. 8) and everyone 'ecclesiastical,' even if the current ecclesiastical law book still always speaks with predilection of clerics as 'ecclesiastici.' Therefore in the church there must be brotherliness, conversation, joint responsibility of all for all, partnership, and dialogue. Consequently even the highest hierarchs are never simply vis-à-vis the community, but at the same time are always fellow Christians, fellow students, fellow servants, as Augustine said, to whom still another service has been entrusted, as a different one has to another person, without, nevertheless, their losing all their fundamental equality."

3. F. Klostermann, *Das Zweite Vatikanische Konzil.*

Konstitutionen, Dekrete und Erklärungen (Freiburg-Basel-Vienna, 1966/67), I, pp. 260–283; II, pp. 585–701.

4. Cf. the recent article by E. Golomb, "Kirchenstruktur Brüderlichkeit," *Wort und Wahrheit* 23 (1968), pp. 291–305.

5. What N. Greinacher says in "Der Vollzug der Kirche im Bistum," in *Handbuch der Pastoraltheologie* III, p. 106, concerning the diocese is valid also for the parish and the universal church: "There often still stands in the way of the realization of brotherliness and collegiality in the diocese a *paternalism* that is profoundly unchristian. For God himself has made an end to paternity on earth—there may yet be a physical, vicarious kind—as his Son entered as our brother into humanity and its history. It is time therefore to make an end to a paternalism that is socially obsolete as well as essentially unchristian. Brotherliness and paternalism in the church are mutually exclusive. The very difficult question arises of whether Christian brotherliness does not slide into the background in the church to the same degree as the notion of the father in reference to the pope, bishops, and priests pushes to the fore. W. Dirks is correct in saying, 'If the Evangelical Church is threatened more by excessive fraternal confusion, in the Catholic Church it is the Father image, the fear of brotherhood, which threatens the Word of Christ in history.' "

6. Cf. the very illuminating article by J. Neumann, "Das 'ius divinum' im Kirchenrecht," in *Orientierung* 31 (1967), pp. 5–8.

7. On apostolic succession, cf. besides the usual works on the church in the New Testament (by O. Linton and F. M. Braun, and the monographs by F. J. Leenhardt, N. A. Dahl, O. Michel, G. Johnston, W. Robinson, A. Oepke, G. Aulén, L. G. Champion, A. Nygren, P. Minear, K. H. Schelkle, R. Schnackenburg, L. Cervaux) the more specialized researches by Ph. H. Menoud, *L'Eglise et le ministère selon le NT* (Neuchâtel, 1949); G. W. H. Lampe, *Some Aspects of the NT Ministry* (London, 1949); H. von Campenhausen, *Kirchliches Amt und geistliche Vollmacht in den ersten drei Jahrhunderten* (Tübingen, 1953); H. Schlier, *Die Zeit der Kirche* (Freiburg i. Br., 1955), pp. 129–147; G. Dix, *Le*

160 NOTES

Ministère dans l'église ancienne (Neuchâtel-Paris, 1955);
E. Schweizer, *Gemeinde und Gemeindeordnung im NT*
(Zürich, 1959); E. Käsemann, *Exegetische Versuche und
Besinnungen* I (Göttingen, 1960), pp. 109–134; H. U. von
Balthasar, *Sponsa Verbi* (Einsiedeln, 1960), pp. 80–147; E.
Schlink, *Der kommende Christus und die kirchlichen Tra-
ditionen* (Göttingen, 1961), pp. 160–195; for literature from
the fields of history and systematic theology on the subject
of ecclesiastical office, see H. Küng, *Structures of the Church*
(Thomas Nelson & Sons, 1964), Ch. VI (includes a response
to the positions of Käsemann and Schlink), and the pertinent
lexicon articles.

8. For the basic foundation of all that follows, see H.
Küng, *The Church* (New York, 1968), Ch. E.

9. Cf. Greinacher, *loc cit.*, pp. 106 f.: "If we are in ear-
nest when we speak of Christian brotherliness and the equality
of the members of the diocese, we must move toward a far-
reaching *democratization of the structures of the church.*
Such a democratization corresponds on the one hand to an
original and genuine stream of Christian tradition in the
church and on the other hand also to the mentality and the
structures of contemporary secular society, which, as we have
shown, cannot conceal its own Christian origins. One thing
must be clear: one cannot speak of the co-responsibility of
the laity if participation in *decision-making* is not granted.
The summons of the laity to co-responsibility and care for
the diocese has meaning really only if this laity is also guaranteed a genuine role in diocesan decision-making. If this is
not the case, then one not unjustly runs the danger that this
summons to joint care will be regarded as a farce. If the
complaint is heard so often that the laity show so slight an
interest in the call to participation in the apostolate, then it
should be asked whether the necessary place has also been
made for their role in decision-making. Only under this condition of genuine participation in decision-making will it be
possible in the long run to integrate the laity into the church
in any authentic way."

10. Peter Stockmeier, *supra,* shows of course that the constitution of the ancient church was very much closer, and
not only just in time, to the original Christian message and

church than was the constitution of the post-Tridentine church.

11. Congar, *Jalons . . .* , pp. 329–333.

12. Küng, *Structures of the Church,* Ch. V.

13. The notions raised here are developed in a more general context in H. Küng, *Truthfulness: The Future of the Church* (Sheed & Ward, Inc., 1968), Chapter B IX.

14. Further possibilities of cooperation between presiding officers and congregation are discussed by A. Müller and R. Völkel, "Die Funktion der Laien in der Pfarrgemeinde," in *Handbuch der Pastoraltheologie* III (Freiburg-Basel-Vienna, 1968), pp. 233–253.

15. On the election of bishops, cf. besides the manuals on the history of canon law (especially E. Feine, Wm. Plöchl), the short summary by K. Mörsdorf in the article "Bischof III. Kirchenrechtlich," in *Lexikon für Theologie und Kirche* II (Freiburg i. Br., 1958), pp. 497–505.

16. Cf. esp. Stockmeier, *supra.*

17. Greinacher, *loc. cit.,* p. 107: "If it is correct that every believing Christian is a brother or sister of Jesus and that the Spirit of Christ operates in each, that the Spirit blows where it will, and that there is also charisma outside office, then the idea cannot be excluded that these Christians should also exert an influence on the fulfillment of the church in the diocese and on the *filling of posts of service.* In the election of the apostle Matthias (Acts 15:22 f.) as well as in the election of deacons (Acts 6:1–6), the collaboration of the entire community was considered self-explanatory (cf. also Acts 15:22 f.). It is well known that the leaders of the congregations in the first centuries up to the time of Ambrose and Augustine were determined with the collaboration of the congregation. Until recently the church tolerated a situation in which the nobility exerted an influence on the filling of certain parish positions. Even up to the year 1903 the church countenanced the fact that in practice the Kaiser influenced the papal elections. Up until our own time—and not only in Eastern countries—the governments in some countries exerted a massive influence on the episcopal elections. Would it not be more appropriate to give some influence in the filling of offices to everyone who is immediately concerned

and who is co-responsible for the bishopric—namely, the members of the local church? Is it not time to give the old democratic tendencies in the church another chance and endow them with a new meaning and a new expression that would be suitable for our time, that is characterized by the process of 'fundamental democratization'?"

VII. PEOPLE, PRIESTS, AND BISHOPS IN U. S. CATHOLIC HISTORY

1. Just how closely linked "Americanism," *Reform-katholizismus,* and "modernism" were in the minds of many Catholics at that time is well exemplified by the work of the conservative Catholic theologian Anton Gisler, *Der Modernismus* (Einsiedeln, 1912). He divided his almost 700-page volume into two parts: Part One, "Forerunners of Modernism"; Part Two, "Genuine Modernism." Part One is further divided into two books, the first of which is entitled "Americanism"; section one is "Americanism in America," section two "Americanism in Europe" (including a chapter entitled "Americanism as Reform Catholicism in Germany"), and section three a detailed analysis and judgment on the Americanist program—222 pages in all.

2. The most thoroughgoing historian of the period, Peter Guilday, stated fifty years ago: "We have yet, however, to be given an impartial history of trusteeism in Carroll's time. The whole question must be treated from another angle from that usually taken, namely the presence of presumptuous, arrogant, and turbulent lay-folks in the congregations where the evil arose." *The Life and Times of John Carroll* (New York, 1922), p. 788. Almost half a century later, Rev. Andrew Greeley wrote: "Unfortunately a careful study of the lay trustee system has not been done and most American Catholics know only of the abuses of the trustee system. Even today when lay participation in parish administration is discussed, it is frequently apt to be dismissed as a return to trusteeism—as though the very use of the word were enough to settle the controversy. Lay trustees are permitted by canon law, and the French-Canadian Church seems to prosper very well under such a system. It was a great historical misfortune that the few schisms which did occur in the United States prevented more experimentation with lay par-

ticipation in Church property administration in this country." *The Catholic Experience* (Doubleday & Company, Inc.,
1967), p. 48.

3. Rev. Gerald C. Treacy, S.J., "Evils of Trusteeism,"
Historical Records and Studies VIII (June, 1915), pp. 136–
156. Robert F. McNamara, "Trusteeism in the Atlantic
States, 1785–1863," *The Catholic Historical Review* XXX,
2 (July, 1944), pp. 135–154.

4. Peter Guilday, "Trusteeism," *Historical Records and
Studies* XVIII (March, 1928), pp. 7–73.

5. Treacy, *loc. cit.,* p. 136.

6. Guilday, *John Carroll,* p. 782.

7. *Ibid.,* pp. 782–783.

8. Peter Guilday, *The Life and Times of John England,*
2 vols. (New York, 1927), Vol. I, pp. 27–28.

9. Guilday, "Trusteeism," p. 13: "The evils which manifested themselves in these churches on a grand scale, were
witnessed in a minor degree in almost every congregation
throughout the country, under the government of lay trustees."

10. Daniel Callahan, *The Mind of the Catholic Layman*
(Charles Scribner's Sons, 1963), p. 21.

11. Letter of Carroll to Cardinal Antonelli, February 17,
1785, quoted in: Annabelle M. Melville, *John Carroll of
Baltimore* (Charles Scribner's Sons, 1955), p. 230.

12. Italics added. Guilday, *John Carroll,* p. 265.

13. *Ibid.,* p. 293.

14. There is an interesting discrepancy between the versions of this letter published by Martin I. J. Griffin ("The
Church of the Holy Trinity, Philadelphia," *Records of the
American Catholic Historical Society of Philadelphia* XXI,
1 [March, 1910], p. 10) and Peter Guilday (*John Carroll,*
p. 293). Griffin wrote: "On the back of this letter Rev. John
Carroll drafted his reply. It has many erasures, but the an-
nexed appears to have been the reply sent." At the end of the
quoted letter Griffin stated: "Here the draft ends. A line
of erasure is drawn down through it. Perhaps this may indi-
cate the letter sent—if one were sent—did not contain all the
words or the sentiment as above set forth. The draft is to be
accepted as simply showing the sentiments of Father Carroll
at the time." The last two sentences of Carroll as quoted by

Griffin are as follows. "Above all things be mindful of charity and brotherly love; avoid contentions; always avoid the usurpation of spiritual powers and every attempt to force on your ecclesiastical Superior Clergymen whom he disapproves. This, in any Country would be hurtful to Religion; in this it would totally destroy it." There is no mention of the phrase about the election of the pastor given in the Guilday version. Guilday's version is as follows, including the ellipsis: "Above all things be mindful of charity and brotherly love, avoid contentions, never assuming the exercise of that power, which can only be communicated to the minister of Christ: let the election of the pastor of your new church be so settled that every danger of a tumultuous appointment be avoided as much as possible. In any country this would be hurtful to religion; in this, it would totally destroy it. . . . As you undertake to raise your church at your own charge and with your own industry, it is possible you may have it in view to reserve to yourselves the appointment of its clergymen, even without the concurrence of the ecclesiastical superior. On this matter I request to hear again from you as I conceive it may involve consequences to religion of the most serious nature." (Guilday's reference was to the Baltimore Cathedral Archives, Case 9-N, 1, 2, 3, 4.) After the quotation Guilday added: "Premir and the committee interpreted this letter as an approval of their project, and the building of the church commenced at once." Guilday refers approvingly to the Griffin article on the page before, but strangely does not comment on the variant versions of the letter of Carroll, nor does he purport to give the letter in full, as Griffin supposedly attempts to do, nor does he say anything at all about Carroll's important statement about the election of the pastor.

15. John Tracy Ellis (ed.), *Documents of American Catholic History* (Bruce Publishing Company, 1956), p. 221.

16. *Ibid.*

17. In the brief to Maréchal, Pius VII stated (August 22, 1822): "There is another circumstance which affords continual cause of discord and contention, not only in Philadelphia, but also in many other places of the United States of America: the immoderate and unlimited right, which trustees or administrators of the temporal properties of churches assume, independently of the diocesan Bishops. Indeed, unless

this be circumscribed by certain regulations, it may prove an eternal source of abuses, and dissensions. . . . But that trustees and laymen should arrogate to themselves the right, as it has sometimes happened in these countries, of establishing as pastors, priests destitute of legal faculties, and even not unfrequently bound by censures (as it appears was lately the case with regard to Hogan), and also of removing them at their pleasure, and of bestowing the revenue upon whom they please, is a practice *new* and *unheard* of in the church." Quoted in Guilday, *John England,* Vol. I, pp. 356–357. When claims were made by trustees to the right to appoint pastors, they based their arguments on the right of patrons, *jus patronatus,* provided for in the then, and still, existing canon law (canons 1448–1471), giving those, for example, who provided the money for the building of a church the right to select in some fashion and present to the bishop the priest to serve there. However, the trustees were most often told that they did not have the *jus patronatus* because certain technicalities were not fulfilled.

18. Guilday, *John England,* Vol. II, p. 125. In 1866, Archbishop Peter Richard Kenrick of St. Louis "objected strongly to the existing practice of accumulating property in the hands of the ordinary and securing it by will. 'I need not say,' he explained, 'that the reputation of great riches, which attaches to most of the Bishops, has the effect of exciting odium against them on the part of non-Catholics, and of indisposing Catholics to contribute freely as they otherwise would towards the wants of the Church.' He preferred a trustee arrangement." David Spalding, "Martin John Spalding, Legislator," *Records of the American Catholic Historical Society of Philadelphia* LXXV, 3 (September, 1964), p. 151.

19. "The trustee system was not an unmitigated evil. Much constructive work was done by zealous laymen, who labored with and under the direction of missionary priests and bishops to establish the Church on a sound financial and material basis. . . . Trusteeism was not the serious problem to the Church in the Old Northwest that it was in other sections of the United States." Alfred G. Stritch, "Trusteeism in the Old Northwest, 1800–1850," *The Catholic Historical Review* XXX, 2 (July, 1944), pp. 157, 161.

20. Cf. Callahan, *op. cit.*, pp. 28–51. In 1855, Archbishop Hughes wrote: "Regarded *a priori,* no system could appear to be less objectionable, or more likely both to secure advantages to those congregations, and at the same time to recommend the Catholic religion to the liberal consideration of the Protestant sentiment of the country. It would, he thought [Archbishop Carroll], relieve the priest from the necessity and painfulness of having to appeal from the altar on questions connected with money, touching either the means of his own support, repairs of the church, or other measures essential to the welfare of his congregation. It would at the same time secure the property, by the protection of law, for the perpetual uses to which it had been set apart and consecrated. It would be a bond of union between the priest and the people. It would be a shield to protect the minister of the altar from the very suspicion of being a money seeker, and at the same time a means to provide for his decent maintenance. All these were no doubt the considerations which moved the venerable and patriotic Archbishop to adopt and recommend the system of Lay trustees. On paper and in theory that system was entirely inobjectionable.

"It was well calculated to gain the confidence of a mind so generous and so liberal as that of the first Archbishop of Baltimore." Quoted in Guilday, "Trusteeism," p. 12. Unfortunately for the American church, Archbishop Hughes and most of his fellow bishops did not choose to promote these admitted beneficial aspects of the lay trustee system.

21. According to England's constitution, a vestry for each of the district churches was to be elected by the members in good standing. The following procedure was set up for complaints against the appointed pastor: "Should the vestry of the district be displeased with the conduct or the proceedings of the clergyman of the same, they shall have power, upon sufficient notice from the secretary, who must issue such notice upon the requisition in writing of two vestrymen, signed by them, to assemble without the clergyman, for the sole purpose of conferring together upon the cause of complaint and of embodying the same in writing; to be immediately transmitted to the bishop or vicar for his judgment thereupon; but which complaint they shall not publish in any other way without the leave, in writing of the bishop or

vicar first being had and obtained therefore." *The Works of the Rt. Rev. John England*, 5 vols., ed. by Ignatius Reynolds (Baltimore, 1849), V, p. 103.

22. Fifteen conventions were held at Charleston for the District of South Carolina (1823–1838). Eight were held at Augusta for the District of Georgia (1826–1835), and two at Fayetteville for the District of North Carolina (1829–1831). Three general conventions of the diocese were held at Charleston, in 1839, 1840, and 1841.

23. Guilday, *John England*, Vol. I, pp. 376–377.

24. Quoted in *ibid.*, Vol. I, p. 376.

25. *Ibid.*, Vol. II, p. 268. There has been a great deal of concern at the present time about the establishment of due process procedures for priests; substantial pressure was put on the American bishops, and consequently in 1969 at the National Conference of Catholic Bishops a set of due process procedures drawn up by the Canon Law Society was adopted. The diocese of Detroit adopted a somewhat similar set of procedures for everyone in the diocese, lay and clerical.

26. *Ibid.*, Vol. II, pp. 268–269.

27. Letter of England to Bishop Rosati of St. Louis, dated Rome, January 14, 1833, quoted in *ibid.*, Vol. II, p. 249.

28. On December 21, 1824, Archbishop Maréchal of Baltimore, England's greatest antagonist, wrote to Rome: "The rumor is abroad that the illustrious Dr. England, Bishop of Charleston, has established a *democratic* constitution by which he intends to govern his diocese, and that he has sent it to the Holy Congregation to have it approved. On which principles it is based I do not know. Nevertheless I cannot properly ask the most holy and eminent fathers to approve this *democratic* constitution, except after a very prolonged and extremely mature examination, for it contains quite a number of things opposed to the welfare and prosperity of the church." Quoted in the Latin original in Guilday, *John England*, Vol. I, pp. 350–351. Of course the word "democratic," which Maréchal underlined, had the same effect in Roman circles at that time as the term "communist" has today in John Birch Society circles.

Just about a week after Archbishop Maréchal's letter, Bishop Conwell of Philadelphia also wrote a bitter denunciation to Rome: "If this Constitution of *democratic* method of

168 NOTES

ruling the Church be approved by the Holy See, it might become necessary to extend it to all the dioceses here, and it would mean the quick collapse of the American Church. The bishop England boasts in his newspaper that part of the Constitution had been sent to Rome for approval, and once that it is granted, it will be proposed to trustees all over America, who with the bishop like a king, and representatives of the laity and the clergy, each year will discuss ecclesiastical affairs. It is to be hoped that the sanction of the Sacred Congregation will be withheld from this, or at least supreme caution be used, for if it were once sanctioned ecclesiastical liberty would end in this country." Conwell to Cardinal-Prefect of Propaganda Fide, January 1, 1825, as quoted in Guilday, *John England,* Vol. I, p. 362.

29. "There is one letter, dated September 14, 1830, from the Cardinal-Prefect to Bishop England, which must have given the latter great joy, for it contains a retraction of the reproof administered to him by Propaganda on August 27, 1825. The Cardinal-Prefect apologized for the severe terms used in the letter and told the Bishop of Charleston that they had been misled at Rome by some who had written against him." *Ibid.,* Vol. I, p. 364.

30. For a somewhat detailed discussion of the implications of this encyclical see: Leonard Swidler, *Freedom in the Church* (Pflaum Press, 1969), pp. 46 ff.

31. Quoted in Guilday, *John Carroll,* p. 348.

32. *Ibid.,* p. 351

33. *Ibid.,* p. 360.

34. *Ibid.,* pp. 568–569.

35. *Ibid.,* pp. 569–570. See also Charles Florence McCarthy, "The Historical Development of Episcopal Nominations in the Catholic Church of the United States (1784–1884)," *Records of the American Catholic Historical Society of Philadelphia* XXXVIII, 4 (December, 1927), pp. 319–320: "On September 29, 1792, Cardinal Antonelli replied to Carroll: 'This Sacred Congregation, His Holiness' will being directly expressed, enjoins your Lordship to take the advice of older and wiser priests of the diocese, and propose a clergyman, one of those in the American mission, who might be fit and acquainted with the affairs, and the Holy Father

would then appoint him coadjutor with the necessary faculties.' " This article by McCarthy was very helpful in the writing of this section of my paper, as was also the article by John Tracy Ellis in the *Critic*, June, 1969.

36. Guilday, *John Carroll*, p. 575.

37. *Ibid.*, p. 591.

38. McCarthy, *loc. cit.*, p. 332.

39. *Ibid.*, p. 334.

40. *Concilia Provincialia Baltimori Habita* (Baltimore, 1851), p. 20.

41. Colman J. Barry, *The Catholic Church and the German Americans* (Bruce Publishing Company, 1953), p. 17.

42. *Concilium Baltimorense Provinciale VIII, habitum anno 1855* (Baltimore, 1857), p. 23.

43. Spalding, *loc. cit.*, p. 151.

44. Callahan, *op. cit.*, p. 44.

45. McCarthy, *loc. cit.*, pp. 347–348.

46. For example, Thomas T. McAvoy, *The Americanist Heresy in Roman Catholicism, 1898–1900* (University of Notre Dame Press, 1963); Robert D. Cross, *The Emergence of Liberal Catholicism in America* (Harvard University Press, 1958); and Daniel Callahan, *The Mind of the Catholic Layman*.

47. Callahan, *op. cit.*, pp. 62–78.

48. Since 1916 each bishop is supposed to consult secretly and individually the diocesan consultors and irremovable pastors every odd-numbered year, and then on his own responsibility suggest one or more names as possible episcopal candidates to the metropolitan. There is no meeting of the priests or representatives of the priests, nor is the bishop obliged to submit any of the names suggested to him.

49. "There are indications in the United States that certain bishops, notably the cardinals and, by the public admission of the present incumbent, the apostolic delegate, have a disproportionate influence in appointments. Because of the development of the system, such persons are likely to recommend only 'safe' candidates and to lay stress upon administrative rather than pastoral or teaching qualifications. Because of the secrecy, it is not known whether the Holy See ever becomes aware of the true situation in regard to

episcopal appointments." "Appointment Procedures for Roman Catholic Bishops," *Herder Correspondence* IV, 4 (April, 1967), p. 116.

50. For example, the middle-of-the-road Jesuit magazine *America* stated: "These nominations made by the bishops, however, still take place in secrecy, and generally with no consultation of the laity or lower clergy. Thus, at the immensely important level of the choice of possible future bishops, the great body of the People of God—including most of their priests—have no voice whatsoever. Indeed, though today a large number of the faithful are knowledgeable about the Church, they feel altogether uninformed about how their bishops are chosen. It is no surprise that they feel left out and belittled, if not insulted. . . . The choice, be it repeated, is not between total secrecy and a full, open plebiscite, which is a rarely used procedure even in a political democracy. Something in between can and should be worked out." *America* 116, 23 (June 10, 1967), p. 827. In the same year the Canon Law Society of America recommended "that there be a restoration of the ancient tradition of an effective participation of the Christian people in the election of their bishops." Quoted in Joseph Menton, "How Do They Choose a Bishop?" *Liguorian* 55, 6 (June, 1967), p. 39.

51. On June 8, 1967, Bishop Primeau of Manchester asked each of the priests of his diocese to submit to him a list of three priests, in order of preference, they considered worthy episcopal candidates, which lists he would use in making his annual suggestions. "The Selection of Bishops," *Priests' Forum* I (March–April, 1969), p. 26. *America* reported that "when Cardinal Joseph Ritter of St. Louis asked his newly established pastoral council (made up of priests, religious and lay people) to give him their recommendations for future bishops, his gesture was hardly radical. A few weeks before, in fact, Bishop Clarence G. Issenmann of Cleveland had called upon each parish to suggest three candidates as possible future bishops." *America* 116, 11 (March 18, 1967), p. 365.